Mining Online Gold with an Offline Shovel

Mining Online Gold with an Offline Shovel

How to Build a Massive Online Mailing List by Mastering Offline Promotion

Joel Christopher and George McKenzie

MASTERMIND LEARNING SYSTEMS

Dr. Bernardo Remandaban
A man of few words with a bias for action,
whose living example of service and dedication showed his son
that making a living by making a meaningful difference
in the lives of others is the key to success and happiness.

and

George McKenzie Sr. and MaryAnn Sebastian McKenzie
Who gave their son love, security, and faith that anything is possible.

Contents

Part 1 : Milking the Media

Chapter 8: Self-Publishing 129

Part 3: Using Low-Cost/High-Return Offline Advertising to Generate Clicks

Chapter 9: Converting Ads to Clicks 149

Part 4: Offline Networking

Foreword
by Jay Conrad Levinson

Although the Internet is still in its infancy, Joel Christopher and George McKenzie manage to bring it closer to adulthood with their insightful, readable, and mind-boggling *Mining Online Gold with an Offline Shovel.*

This book removes the mystique from online marketing and shows readers how it is simpler than they may imagine. Rather than expound upon theories and old-fashioned thinking, this book delves into truths, and does it with state-of-the-moment thinking.

Just reading this book and embracing its concepts will make the difference between dismal failure and rip-roaring success for many an online entrepreneur — regardless of the size of their business.

As many masters do, Joel and George take a very complex idea and present it in the most simple and understandable terms. Their book is hardly a get-rich-quick book, but it is most assuredly a get-rich-for-certain book. Loaded with real-life examples, it offers practical, honest, and profit-producing advice — the kind you can take to the bank.

Perhaps most surprising of all, this book does not tell you anything that you expect it to tell you. It is filled with wise counsel that you haven't read elsewhere, haven't heard elsewhere, and probably didn't know. I've written 30 books, three of them about online marketing, and I learned a lot in every chapter.

Joel and George mention names, tell specific numbers, give websites, hide nothing behind esoteric prose, and do it in a warm and engaging style. It this book as captivating as a best-selling novel? It is if you want to earn a ton of money using the Internet.

In this book, expect the unexpected. Expect to be enlightened. Expect to learn things you never dreamed were possible. And expect to get onto a first-name basis with your banker because of the regular and sizeable deposits you'll be making.

You probably grew up hearing "Sticks and stones may break my bones, but names will never hurt me." Now, that adage may be revised to "Sticks and stones may break my bones, and opt-in names will definitely help me."

The authors do not make the path to online wealth sound easy, but they do make it seem possible. Blending classic common sense with brand new marketing technology, *Mining Online Gold with an Offline Shovel* ought to be mandatory reading for anyone with even the glimmer of hope of earning a fortune on the Internet.

It covers all, and I mean *all* the bases. It guides readers step-by-step towards their goals. My only regret about the book is that Joel and George didn't write it ten years ago when I began my own foray into online marketing.

If I only knew then what they've taught me now!

Jay Conrad Levinson
Author, *Guerrilla Marketing* series of books
Over 14 million sold; now in 39 languages

170 Seaview Drive
San Rafael, California
94901
Tel: (415) 453-2162
Fax: (415) 456-2701
Email: Jayview@aol.com
Web: www.jayconradlevinson.com, www.gmarketing.com

Mining Online Gold with an Offline Shovel

Introduction

Digging for Internet Gold

You've probably heard the stories... but you probably didn't believe them.

You've got to admit, there are dozens — make that hundreds — of can't-miss, guaranteed, get-rich-quick ideas and offers that show up in your email box every week.

At best, most of it is hype. At worst, it's outright fraud.

But the verifiable truth is you can make more money on the Internet, in less time, with less effort, than with any other enterprise in human history (with the possible exception of the Powerball lottery).

It can be like striking gold. One minute you're just another prospector scratching around in the hills... a day later you can have more money in your bank account than most people make in five years.

How can that be possible?

Through the power of email, that's how.

Through the power of a list of people who "opt in" to your newsletter, allowing you to contact them, on a regular basis, over and over again.

In fact, you don't even have to have a newsletter. All you need is a list of people who have said, in effect, "When you've got something to sell that I might be interested in buying, tell me about it via email."

Your opt-in list is your gold mine.

3

Here are some examples of how several extremely savvy marketers have used their opt-in lists to strike Internet gold.

On May 24, 2000, Houston entrepreneur and author Robert Allen challenged himself to make $24,000 in twenty-four hours by mailing an offer to his ten thousand subscribers.

Orders poured in. Twenty-four hours later, he had not only surpassed the twenty-four thousand dollar target, he nearly quadrupled it.

$90,000 in one day.

March 10, 2001. Terry Dean of Indiana—who had been delivering pizzas just a few years before—sent an email offer to his list of about thirty-three thousand.

Sixty-seven people bought the deal. It doesn't sound like much, but when you consider that the product he sold cost $495… Well, you do the math.

Our calculator says that's $33,165 dollars.

From a single email.

In 2002, Terry emailed a similar offer to his list, which had grown to more than fifty thousand by then.

This time his take was $71,000 in a single day.

Our favorite story, though, involves Bob Gatchell.

Gatchell didn't even have a product to sell, but he did control an opt-in list. He set up a partnership with someone who had created a home study course that cost about $500. He offered the home study course to his subscribers.

Bob later wrote a book based on the results. The book was entitled *How I Made $34,000 Selling a Product I Didn't Create, I Didn't Touch, Someone Else Delivered, While I Sat In A Hot Tub Naked With My Wife!*

Again, your opt-in list is your gold mine.

Why Every Name is a Nugget

Early in 2002, many of the most successful Internet marketers gathered in Hawaii for an event called Internet Marketing Summit. Three of the pioneers of Internet marketing were there: Jonathan Mizel, Stephan Mahaney and Corey Rudl.

Someone asked them "If there were a fire in your office, what one thing would you make sure to take with you as you headed out the door?"

All of them agreed their opt-in list—their database of email subscribers—was the thing that would be most devastating to lose.

In fact, Corey Rudl told the audience that he has a clause in his employees' contracts: if one of them shares or steals his list, he can sue them for 25 million dollars.

Corey has about one million names on his list. So, in other words, he believes each subscriber is worth about 25 dollars.

You can contact these subscribers repeatedly—they've given you permission—and you can sell to them, theoretically, for the rest of their lives.

During that time, they may buy hundreds of dollars worth of products or services from you.

That's what Internet marketers mean when they say "the lifetime value of a visitor."

The great Internet marketers are not those who "take the money and run," selling one product, one time, and then disappearing into cyberspace.

The great Internet marketers turn their website visitors into buyers, and their buyers into lifetime customers—sometimes worth thousands of dollars each.

They do it by persuading those buyers to sign up for their lists.

Do you see now why it's so important to build your list if you expect to make a good living off the Internet?

Purpose of This Book

This book was written to help Internet entrepreneurs attract subscribers to their opt-in lists — subscribers who will buy from them over and over again. Subscribers who will guarantee those entrepreneurs a flow of profits every month, whether they're sitting in front of their computer... or naked in a hot tub with a spouse.

But there's a difference between this book and others on the same subject.

Before now, most books on "list-building" have focused on recruiting customers through online methods: swapping ads, writing articles, or optimizing your website so it will rank high in search engines. When you use these methods, you get subscribers because they've clicked through to your website from somewhere else on the Net.

We'll show you, however, to find new subscribers through methods that have usually been ignored or undervalued by many Internet marketers: offline methods like direct mail, fax broadcasts, teleseminars, attending live workshops and similar events, and free publicity in the mass media.

Our friend Alex Mandossian (www.marketingwithpostcards. com) calls it "bricks and clicks" marketing.

> Very simply, 'bricks' are 'brick and mortar', or physical, marketing methods. The real world. Direct mail, postcards, the telephone. Anything that deals in the non-virtual.

> 'Clicks' are virtual. They don't exist. They're electronic. When you have a website, you don't have physical space. [Your site] is on a server, which takes up physical space, but it's virtual. And when something is virtual, there's less of an experience. You can't touch it, you can't curl up on your couch and highlight it, you can't listen to it.

> If there were email that was scratch and sniff, I'd be the first to raise my hand and get it. But all the senses aren't involved, so when you add bricks and clicks, then you have a marketing model.

The idea of offline marketing to create an online database is not new. It's just that very few people do it. And what I'm talking about are offline techniques like postcards and business reply cards, and fax broadcasts, and catalog booklets and direct mail and refund letters and space ads and using the telephone, and handouts at a seminar, and even teleseminars.

Alex emphasizes that there's really nothing new about a lot of his marketing ideas — it's just that they're now being used with a different goal in mind.

Turning bricks into clicks.

Does Alex know what he's talking about?

Well, consider this. Alex has less than five thousand people on his email list. And each day he gets fewer than 125 visitors to his site.

However, each month for the last nine months of 2002, he made more than $10,000 a month in profit from his website. In several months he made more than $30,000.

It's probably some of the offline marketing that's responsible for that. Going offline is probably the single most important way for now and in the future to develop an online database because it ain't getting any better. With all the spamming filters, and all the other things, we can't even get a message to a friend!

I have to use 'brick' marketing just to communicate with my customers, and it's a travesty.

I'm also sure that sometime in the future, email is going to cost something.

So offline is marketing is here, and it's here to stay.

The mission of this book then, is this: we'll show you how to turn "bricks" into "clicks" and "clicks" into cash.

Why Are "Bricks" Important?

As Alex Mandossian stressed, online marketing is one-dimensional. It's visual. So the online marketing experience usually involves only one of the senses. And you don't have to have passed Psychology 101 to know that the more senses involved in an experience, the more vivid the experience.

That applies to selling too. The more senses involved in the selling process, the more likely the selling process will lead to a sale.

"Bricks" also convey a message of credibility.

Anyone can put up a website — and then hide behind it, faceless and possibly even nameless.

How many times have you scrolled up and down a web page, squinting as you tried to find a phone number you could call to talk to a real person?

How many times have you sent an email to a company doing business on the web and gotten an impersonal "canned" response via autoresponder? A response that probably didn't even answer the question you asked?

"Brick" marketing methods are real. Someone has taken time, made an effort, and possibly even spent a little cash to try to build a relationship with you.

Relationships turn buyers into lifetime customers.

The Biggest Myth About Internet Marketing

A few pages ago, we talked about people who had made huge sums of money, literally overnight, through Internet marketing.

You may have heard names like Declan Dunn, Marlon Sanders, Frank Garon and a number of others who went from relative obscurity to fabulous wealth.

But you probably haven't heard the entire truth about them — "the rest of the story," as Paul Harvey would say.

Declan Dunn created a digital book called "Winning The Affiliate Game." It took him forty-five days to write.

Forty-five days after he put it on the net, he had sold a thousand copies. At $97 dollars a copy.

What's the rest of the story?

Declan Dunn personally telephoned every one of the one thousand people who bought his product.

Do you suspect they were impressed? Do you suspect a large number of them quickly went from one-time buyer to lifetime customer?

Marlon Sanders was probably the first person to sell an electronic, or digital information product on the subject of Internet marketing. Thousands of people worldwide have bought Marlon's Amazing Formula product, available at www.get-free-publicity.com/amazing.html, and used it to successfully build their Internet business. Marlon enjoys one of the highest incomes of anyone doing business on the Internet.

Yet he has an organized follow-up system of personal contact through telephone and direct mail when anyone buys one of his products.

Frank Garon is known around the Internet as "the former bankrupt New Jersey truck driver who now makes more than $100,000 a year through Internet marketing."

Frank has eighteen thousand subscribers to his Internet marketing newsletter, "The Planetgram," but he's quick to point out:

> It's not the size of the list that counts. It's your relationship to the people on that list. Are you real to them? Can they trust what you tell them? Have you given them a reason to believe what you say?

Frank has turned his website, www.internetcashplanet.com into one of the Internet's biggest moneymakers. And he's done it by branding himself as "just another guy who used to drive an eighteen wheeler and making $14.25 an hour."

He has bonded with his subscribers through sometimes humorous, sometimes profound, but always intensely personal newsletters. "Sometimes my readers want to slap me," Frank says. "Sometimes they want to give me a kiss on the cheek. But they read me and buy from me because I've worked hard to build up a relationship. They know I'm a real person.

Why "Offline" Customers Are Often Better Customers

That kind of personal connection converts to dollars in other ways too.

We've found in our own businesses that offline customers who join our lists because of personal contact—telephone, seminars, postcards, and workshops—tend to spend more and complain less.

They're usually more committed, more serious, more passionate, more willing to spend money to reach their goals.

They require less "hand-holding" because they're usually self-motivated and self-sufficient. They're not looking for magic bullet solutions, and they understand that success is a long-term process, not an overnight miracle.

And they spend larger amounts of money over longer periods of time.

And that's what you're in business for, right?

Bricks to clicks.

Clicks to cash.

That's what this book is about.

Part 1
Milking the Media

Chapter 1

Drive in Traffic, Drive Up Sales, Maybe Even Make Yourself Rich and Famous

Advertising.

Publicity.

Ask the average TV viewer, radio listener, or newspaper reader, "What's the difference?" and they'd probably say, "There isn't one. They're both the same thing."

But they're not. Not by a long way. And knowing the difference can put a lot of money in your pocket. Not knowing the difference can mean taking a lot out with little in return.

Here's are some examples:

Recently the San Antonio Express News ran a story about some new software that had just hit the market. Darrin Schroeder, Vice President of a small local company that had just rolled out a similar product, called the reporter and offered a "follow-up."

Result: front page story, with a color picture, in the business section several days later.

Here's another example.

Linda Finstad of www.hatsbyemmanuel.com got a terrific Christmas present recently: a high-profile story, including a color picture, in her local newspaper. Here's how she tells it.

> I have had remarkable success with just one press release idea.

I am a hat designer—you can check out my specialty head-wear at www.hatsbyemmanuel.com

Due to a desire to keep the kids safe at night and to produce a unique product I designed a line of winter hats that incorporate Scotchlite™ reflective strips from 3M.

Because this was is a brand new product it was 'newsworthy'.

Also I made them for kids—always a hit with newspaper reporters.

The product was timely and of interest to a large section of the public.

I wrote a press release sent it off to our local newspaper.

They ran a story and even sent a photographer over to take pictures.

(Editor's note: To see a picture of the newspaper headline and article, visit www.get-free-publicity.com/finstad.htm).

This was great exposure and did increase sales at the 'Old Strathcona Farmers Market' where I sell my hats every Saturday.

However the piece won me more than exposure. I in turn emailed the article to 3M, the makers of the reflective strip, who thought it was a great way to use their product and in turn placed a huge order. They bought hats and headbands featuring the reflective strip for all their employees and gave them out at their Christmas party.

They have also indicated that they would like to buy more in the New Year to use as promotional give-aways.

Linda Finstad

Owner/Designer

Hats By Emmanuel

www.hatsbyemmanuel.com

Both these success stories resulted from a single phone call or press release. Both generated thousands of dollars worth of free publicity… without a dime being spent on advertising.

And that's the difference between advertising and publicity. Any one in the media will be happy to sell you advertising.

Publicity is free.

In other words, as folks like to say in the public relations business, "Advertising is what you pay for. Publicity is what you pray for."

The goal of this section of our book is to show you how your publicity prayers can be answered.

Why Free Publicity is Important to List-Building

There are plenty of marketing studies that have shown you need at least 7 to 10 positive contacts with a prospect before they'll trust you enough to buy from you.

When you capture a subscriber on the Internet, you very rarely sell them anything right away. They have to get to know you, like you, and trust you before they'll punch their credit card number into an order form.

But positive publicity in the mass media can put the know-like-trust cycle onto a fast track.

Paul Hartunian, the man who "sold the Brooklyn Bridge" calls it the "Halo Effect."

> The huge bonus of publicity, is when you get a story written about your website in a newspaper, or if you're interviewed on radio or TV about your website, you get the implied endorsement of that medium. For example, if the Wall Street Journal does a story about your website, people reading that story assume that the Wall Street Journal is endorsing that website. That is extremely powerful. Even if you have a tiny little local website, you want huge publicity. You want an article in USA Today, in the Wall Street Journal, in the New York Times. And all of those are very, very possible.

Publicity is important for another reason.

Most people who are starting to build an Internet business have little or no money for advertising. So free publicity, especially in the mass media, can give a "newbie" thousands of dollars worth of exposure without any cash outlay at all.

Free publicity can turbo-charge your marketing and even result in thousands of dollars worth of sales in a single day

Two more stories will serve as further proof.

Tom Antion (www.antion.com) is a successful professional speaker and seminar leader who teaches presentation and public-speaking skills.

Tom drops everything when the media calls, and his desire to help people in the media do their jobs recently led to a huge freelance contract with, of all things, a media giant.

Here how Tom tells the story.

> *I publish three electronic magazines—or e-zines. After you get thousands of subscribers, you don't really know who's on your list... there's just lots of people who are on your list.*
>
> *Well, a lady was a columnist for a major newspaper in Miami... I forget which one, I think it was the Sun-Sentinel... and she was on my list. She got a question from one of her readers about the Internet. She knows I talk about that a lot in my magazine, so she calls me up and interviews me no more than five minutes, and I forgot all about it.*
>
> *Well, apparently, she printed the answer and in the meantime, CBS was looking for a spokesperson. They're the owner of one of the largest websites in the world, called Switchboard.com. They had a PR firm looking for a spokesperson looking for small business people getting on the Internet. I'm sure they had thousands of people trying for this slot, but I was the one who could speak, because they wanted me to speak to small business people, and I was credible because I really did sell on the Internet... I wasn't just reading it out of a book.*

So the circle came right around from a free magazine...
somebody read something about me. They called... I an-
swered. I know I went out of my way to grab that phone call
and dropped everything just to help that lady out once and
it turned into a contract worth over $100,000 for only three
months. So it can be very, very lucrative!

To check out Tom Antion's "Speaker Shop" a resource center for anyone who wants to present themselves to the media, or to audiences of
any size, visit www.get-free-publicity.com/speakershop.htm

To subscribe to Tom's e-zine, "Great Speaking," go to www.get-free-
publicity.com/antionsubscribe.html

You may have seen Tom recently on MSNBC. Because of his media
marketing skills... and because he's worked hard to become known
as a "hot interview on the media circuit" he was chosen to cri-
tique President Bush's skills as a speaker. His single appearance on
MSNBC resulted in thousands of dollars worth of product sales in
just a few days, and also resulted in hundreds of new subscribers to
his electronic magazine "Great Speaking."

Bart Baggett is also a professional speaker, but he's best known as
one of the foremost authorities on handwriting in the world. He's
a frequent guest on news programs and cable networks who call on
him to analyze handwriting of both the famous and the infamous...

Bart estimates that he's been a guest on about 1500 radio programs
during his career... but none had the impact of a single program
with New York Shock Jock Howard Stern...

Bart described the encounter, and the results, this way.

Howard Stern is one of the biggest radio shows I've ever
been on as a guest. And by the time I did his show, I'd been
on about 700 shows, so I knew what I was doing. But you
never know what Howard Stern is going to say. That show is
basically done by telephone...

He didn't let me do 'my' show. He didn't let me say my nor-
mal jokes and my normal show. He gave me writing samples
of show members and didn't tell me who was who and

they guessed who was who. Long story short, after thirty minutes, he actually gave my 800 number for me. He liked me so much, he said, 'Bart, what's that 800 number again? How can they get hold of you?' I said... 1-800... whatever the number was. Sure enough, we made about $25,000 that morning. That's a nice number for a small business.

That was probably our best day ever as far as radio sales. We've had good days since then, but you're talking 3,000,000 listeners. There's really nothing comparable to that.

Learn more about Bart Baggett's Handwriting Analysis Course at www.get-free-publicity.com/handwriting.html

A Six-fold Traffic Increase from One Press Release

David Frey of www.marketingbestpractices.com publishes a marketing newsletter that reaches more than forty thousand readers. He offers several products and consulting services, and he promotes both by offering his expertise to the media through press releases.

David is a big believer in the power of free publicity. Here's why.

I'll give you a good example of what I've done with press releases. When I think about press releases, the first thing is that they're free. And so usually when you're talking about offline list generation strategies there's always some type of cost involved in them. However, using press releases you can do it for free.

And the objective is to get them to contact you asking for further information (about the subject of the press release).

So I have a website called www.makethegrade.com and it sells programs to parents of high school students, on how to help your children make better grades in school.

So what I did was develop a press release that gave about six or seven different hints as to how to prepare for college. And I sent it out in August, which is the month that many of

the college kids go back to school and the parents' help their children get ready to go back to college.

So the timing of my releases was important. And inside the release, I offered a checklist of things that parents would need to do or should consider when sending their children back to school. That checklist probably consisted of about 50 different things. And I made it available to the readers of the press release by putting it into an auto responder, so all the readers would have to do is send an email to checklist@make thegrade.com and the auto responder would send the check-list right back to them.

Little did they know that I was capturing their email address as well.

And so after the checklist went back to them, then that same auto responder a couple days later would start sending in-formational advertisements or editorial type advertisements through email to the people who responded to or asked for the checklist. And this same strategy can be done in just about any small business.

David's web traffic jumped 600% after his press release went out!

Can You Get Similar Results?

The best thing about getting free publicity from the media is that the process is very democratic. Anybody can do it, as long as they know:

- What the media needs
- Who to approach with ideas or "pitches."
- How to approach them

That's what we'll look at in the next three chapters.

Chapter 2

What the Media Needs from You

'Publicity is the art of making something newsworthy out of something ordinary, or nothing at all... '

Mary Ann Baugh in <u>Power Publicity</u> (with Rick Beneteau)

Imagine yourself sitting down in a meeting room to listen to a presentation by a speaker.

The speaker begins by saying. "Statistics show...." She then proceeds to reel off a list of figures aimed at making a point. Before long though, you'll probably be thinking about all the other places you'd rather be.

Now imagine the speaker begins by saying "Once upon a time... "

You automatically start paying attention because you know you're about to hear a story.

People love stories. And they'll stop what they're doing if they think they're going to hear a good one.

The greatest teachers of all time have taught their lessons through stories, anecdotes, and examples. Even parables.

And you'll start getting loads of free publicity from the media if you understand that they're really in the storytelling business.

The Most Common Mistake
Publicity-Seekers Make

Joan Stewart is a former newspaper reporter and editor with more than 20 years experience. She says that during her career, she got hundreds of calls from people saying, in so many words, "Cover me, pay attention to me, give me publicity…"

Of course, what they really wanted was free advertising for some product they were selling. And when Joan would ask, politely of course, why the public would want to know more about it, they'd launch into details about how wonderful their product was and all the features it offered.

Among professional sales people, this is called "selling features instead of benefits."

Among news decision-makers this is called, "selling the store, not the story."

In other words, people who want publicity often try to sell their product (the *store*), when they should be trying to sell a *story* connected to their product.

Frank Guerra, a former TV reporter, assignment editor, and news executive, tells the following story. At the time, he was the assignment editor at KENS TV in San Antonio, Texas.

By the way, if you don't know what an assignment editor is, see the next chapter.

Frank got a call from a man who had founded a small company, which was celebrating its tenth anniversary at the time. The man "pitched" Frank on the idea of doing a story about their anniversary celebration.

Frank was about to politely turn the request down when the man mentioned something that grabbed Frank's attention.

The man said he was also celebrating his 20th high school reunion at around the same time and that he had been voted "Least Likely To Succeed" by his class.

Now here, Frank thought, is a good human-interest story.

Result: The man and his company got several minutes of free TV exposure worth literally thousands of dollars.

What makes a story "sellable?" More on that later.

For now, just understand that getting media coverage on any given day is something of a crapshoot. But you'll increase your chances enormously if you offer the media stories that hold value for the reader.

"What's It to Me?"

No doubt you've heard the classic analogy that explains the nature of news. "When dog bites man, it's not news. When man bites dog, it's news."

It's a massive oversimplification, but it's essentially correct. Anything that's out of the ordinary, or the opposite of what you expect, is inherently interesting.

But there's another element that is also extremely important: relevance.

Journalists constantly ask themselves this question: how many people need to know, or would like to know this information?

The information has to have some relevance or importance to the audience. That's called "news value."

In other words, you take the viewer's perspective on every story. The viewer, consciously or sub-consciously, always wants to know "What's it to me?" and "Why should I care?"

Pretend that you're a reader, listener, or viewer. Ask yourself those questions whenever you're looking for free publicity from the media.

But right now you might be thinking, "Well, then I've got a problem. I'd like to get some publicity for my child's Little League team, our church's spaghetti dinner, or even a lost pet. Not much news value in those. Does that mean I'm out of luck?"

Not at all. Because there's a saying in the news business: "There are no dull stories. Just dull approaches to interesting stories."

The key is to find a way to make your "dull" story more interesting. In other words, more newsworthy.

Give it some news value.

And there are ways to do that.

Universal News Themes, Story Lines, Hooks and Angles

It's conventional wisdom in the news business that certain things are automatic attention-getters. They're universal themes, story lines, hooks and angles. Let's call them "hot buttons".

Construct your pitch so that it punches one or more of these hot buttons, and you're on your way to thousands — maybe even millions — of dollars worth of free publicity.

The definitions that follow are among the most common, but the list certainly isn't all-inclusive. There's always room for creativity.

Beating the Odds
Any story about someone who has accomplished the unlikely is inherently interesting. A story about someone who's attempting to accomplish something unlikely is also interesting, as long as it's not totally ridiculous (e.g. sending a news release about your client who plans to shoot himself out of a cannon and land on the moon will get tossed in the trash.)

Celebrities
This one's pretty obvious. If we weren't naturally interested in movie stars and sports heroes, there wouldn't be racks full of magazines and tabloids dedicated to them. Anything that has to do with a celebrity automatically gets media attention.

Civic & Charity Connected
News people generally want to project an image that they're concerned citizens with a social conscience. Therefore they look for stories about civic involvement and charity events.

Contests
Everyone does Halloween costume contests, but you can be imagina-

tive and creative at other times of the year. Example: if you owned a restaurant, you could ask your customers to submit stories about their biggest holiday meal disasters, with the winners (pick more than one) getting a free family dinner at your place. Circulate a news release to the media with an invitation to come to your location the night the winners will be there.

For a terrific resource on how to attract media attention with contests, get Joan Stewart's *Special Report #18: Clever Contests That Will Tempt Reporters to Call* at www.get-free-publicity.com/publicityhound.html

Controversy
Again, it's conventional wisdom in the news business that "heat sells better than light." In other words, controversy gets nearly everyone's attention.

"Conspiracy Theory"
As the guardians of the common good, news people are always on the lookout for scams, con games, and "conspiracies" aimed at the public. If you can make even a relatively reasonable case that somebody's out to take advantage of somebody else, you'll probably be able to get the media's attention… especially if it's somebody "big" trying to stick it to somebody "small."

David vs. Goliath
Everyone roots for the underdog, so stories of this sort are a "gimme." There doesn't even have to be an element of conflict—as long as you show how the "little guy," working alone or with minimal resources, has accomplished something the "big guys" with lots of money and power couldn't figure out how to do.

Environment
Clean air, clean water, preserving and protecting natural resources and the overall health of Mother Earth. This one is fairly obvious.

Fighting City Hall
We've also heard the phrase, "You can't fight City Hall." But some people try, and some even succeed. They make interesting stories.

Again though, the fight has to have some basis in reality. There are a lot of kooks running around making all sorts of bizarre claims about their government, and they love to share their fantasies with folks in the media. So if you're going to use this approach, be prepared to demonstrate you're not just a crackpot.

Follow-Ups

Everyone likes "where are they now" stories, right? That's one type of "follow-up," but there are several others. Basically a follow-up is a technique of adding new information to something that's already been in the news. For instance, if some people in your area lost their homes due to flooding, the local newspaper might want to do a follow-up story a few months later telling how those people have been managing.

"God & Country"

Many people are religious and patriotic. Anything that touches on these subjects tends to get attention. But because they're such emotional issues, you really have to be careful how you use them when approaching the media. Don't be crass.

Health and Medical Issues

Almost every TV newscast, almost every newspaper does at least one story related to health and medicine every day.

Holiday Tie-Ins

Stories about firecracker safety on the Fourth of July, how to bake a better Thanksgiving turkey, gift shopping at Christmas time etc.

Human Interest

The greatest teachers of all time have taught their lessons through stories, anecdotes, examples, and even parables. And you'll start getting loads of free publicity from the media if you understand that they're really in the storytelling business.

Kids & Animals

We've all heard that "cute kids and talking dogs are a tough act to follow." Pets and kids are inherently interesting to people.

Local Angle

Offer a local twist on a national story. If you see something on *The Today Show* that touches on your area of expertise, send a quick news release to the NBC affiliate in your town and offer them a "local angle" on the story.

Lost Opportunities

These are stories that tell people they're missing out on something. People like to learn about anything that makes life more convenient, interesting, rewarding, financially secure etc.

Milestones, Firsts, and Record Breaking Events

These are so obvious, we don't need to do anything other than mention them.

Money and Financial or "Pocketbook" Issues

Another "gimme," like environment, health, human-interest stories and milestones.

Myth-Busting

Information that debunks a myth or flies in the face of conventional wisdom will raise eyebrows — and get attention. When you can get talk show hosts and reporters to say, "Wow. I had no idea…" they'll be standing in line to tell your story.

Polls and Surveys

Conduct a survey among your customers, and offer the results to the media. Even surveys asking basic questions like "What's the number one reason you'll stop patronizing a restaurant?" can turn into a filler story on a slow news day. Write and circulate a news release detailing the results.

Technology

Got a great new gizmo that will help speed up service or make life more convenient for your customers? Let the local media know about it, and offer to show them how it works. Example: when some restaurants started taking to-go orders by email.

Because you're in the business, some technological changes may seem basic and everyday to you, but they have a "gee whiz" quality to consumers and reporters. So it's often worth a news release to your local media.

Tip Lists

David Letterman made the idea of a "Top Ten" list famous, and you can get attention by offering the media some lists of your own. Unlike Letterman they don't have to be funny, but they should be interesting, relevant, timely, and if possible, attention-grabbing. For instance, a restaurant might offer: "Five Ways To Make 'Em Love Turkey Leftovers." A cleaning company or maid service can provide "Five Reasons Why There Are More Germs In Your Kitchen Than In Your Bathroom."

Travel
Lots of people are doing it, especially in summer.

Trends or "Signs Of The Times" Stories
These often overlap with stories about new technology. They're examples of trends and innovations.

Vanity
A powerful human emotion and therefore a possible source of stories. Anything that helps people look better or feel smarter creates interest.

Weather
It affects just about everybody, just about every day. Therefore it can be newsworthy. This category would also include seasonal and climate-related stories.

"Whoa's" and "Over the top" stuff
If this kind of story didn't get attention, the circus would have gone out of business long ago. It doesn't have to be weird, but anything that's unusual or "eye-popping" will work.

Caution: Hot Buttons Are Often in the "Eye of the Beholder"

Have you ever sat in front of your TV, watching a local newscast, and said to yourself, "I don't like that news anchor. There's just something that bothers me"?

Most of the time, it has nothing to do with that person's professional qualifications or congeniality. You just don't like their looks, their voice, or the way they raise an eyebrow when they say certain words. Or maybe they remind you of a high school classmate you disliked.

That's called a subjective judgment, right?

In a sense, that happens with news judgment too. You may send a news release to one place and it goes in the trash. The same release goes to another place and they nearly trip on themselves trying to get you aired or published.

Subjective judgment. Period.

Journalists in every medium watch their competition. They'll debate at length whether a particular story should have been "page 1 above the fold" or "page 2 below the fold." They pick apart each other's writing styles, and fuss over the way someone spent too much time talking about one part of the story and not enough talking about another.

It's all about human nature and subjective judgment. The news business is as much art as science, and therefore, everyone's opinion is as good as anyone else's.

So don't waste a lot of time and energy feeling good about the success of one news release or feeling bad about the failure of another. Use the experience to learn anything you think might be useful, and get to work cranking out other releases.

Stick as best you can to the principles in this book. Don't be afraid to take a chance. Don't sweat bullets over small stuff in your release, and don't fret about splitting semantic hairs.

Most important of all, just keep getting your ideas in front of people.

Keep pushing those hot buttons.

Success will come.

Chapter 3
Media Decision-Makers: Who Calls the Shots — and Why You Need to Know

In sales, you always want to be able to make your pitch to the person who makes the buying decision, right?

The same is true with the media.

But who makes the "buying decision" in a radio, TV, or newspaper newsroom?

MDMs, that's who. Media Decision-Makers — the people who make choices about what to cover and not to cover.

And there's one thing that's absolutely critical to understand about them.

The Clock is Always Ticking

Before we tell you who the key players are in the news business, let's talk about how they live their daily professional lives.

Here's an example you can probably relate to.

Imagine that you had lunch with an important client or prospect. You thought you had plenty of time, but the client or prospect got chatty, the restaurant was jammed and service was slow.

It's now about 1:45 and you're due back at the office for an important two o'clock meeting. You can't afford to be late. If you hit the traffic lights just right, you'll walk into the conference room right on time.

But you don't hit the first couple of lights just right, and you're start-ing to sweat.

Then at 1:55, half a mile from the office, you see the blocking arms coming down just as you're pulling up to a the train crossing. A freight train lumbers into view.

Now you're really sweating about being late.

Ever had that feeling? Not fun, huh?

That's the feeling most people in the news business live with. Not just once in a while either.

Every day.

Unless you've been through it, you can't imagine the gut-wrenching that goes on as a deadline approaches and you're battling to get your column written, your radio report ready, or your TV live shot on the air.

Newspaper folks have it tough enough. But electronic journalists know that they face the constant possibility they may have to go on the air without being fully prepared—and that they may be about to make an idiot of themselves in front of a couple hundred thousand people.

There are constant challenges.

Journalistic
Is your information accurate? Have you confirmed it? Is there any-thing important you're leaving out? Will your competition have something you don't?

Human
There are other people screwing up their jobs all around you, but you still have to get yours done as if everything and everyone performed flawlessly.

Technical
Computers crash. Cameras and tape recorders don't work. Tires go flat. Technological advances in newsgathering have been breathtak-ing the last three decades. But one thing hasn't changed: Murphy's Law.

Throw all these challenges together, and simply doing your job everyday can get fairly uncomfortable.

When you're dealing with the media, it's important for you to understand the mindset of the people you'll be dealing with.

And the mindset is "get to the point, tell me what I need to know, and don't waste my time with anything unnecessary."

In other words, if it's important, say it fast. If it's not, say it later."

That's a great rule to remember when you're pitching a reporter or crafting a press release.

Make it Easy On Them, and You'll Make it Profitable for Yourself

Here's how you can use the constant "crunch time" mindset to your advantage.

You do it by dealing with the media in a way that makes it easy for them to figure out, almost instantly, if you have something worthy of attention.

In other words, you make their job easy for them.

Knowing that journalists almost always *feel* like they're in a hurry, even when they're really not, you do them a great favor by keeping things painfully simple, short, and clear.

They appreciate it. More importantly, they respond favorably to it.

That said, let's go over some job descriptions of people you'll be dealing with.

They go by different names in different places, so once again, from now on we'll collectively refer to them as MDMs — Media Decision-Makers.

Who's In Charge?

Producing a newscast, a radio show, a newspaper or a magazine resembles putting on a stage production. The actors do their jobs in front of the audience; they get nearly all the glory and much of the money.

But behind the scenes, someone else is really calling the shots—the director and the producer.

It's pretty much the same in the news business.

The folks you see on screen, the people whose voices you hear on radio, the writers whose names appear in bylines beneath the headlines—often have little to do with deciding what gets covered. Generally it's pointless to direct your efforts to them (there are exceptions, though, which we'll cover below).

The real power is usually in the hands of people who work quietly and often anonymously far away from the front page or the on-air side of the camera.

These are the people you want to get to know.

We'll spend more time in the chapters that follow on *how* to pitch, but for now let's just look at some basic job titles of people you're likely to bump into as you market yourself to the media.

Before we do though, one suggestion.

It's never a bad idea to call the main switchboard at any news outlet and get some intelligence. Just ask the simple question.

"If I wanted to suggest that someone cover a story about _____, whom should I talk to?"

Don't forget to make sure you ask for a correct spelling and pronunciation of that person's name.

Print Media

Editor
The important thing to remember about the job title "editor" is this: the job description that accompanies the title generally depends on the size of the publication.

You'd be wasting your time pitching a story to the editor of the New York Times.

But pitching the editor of a small town weekly is a different story.

It's a judgment call, and requires some intelligent research on your part.

Generally, it's counter-productive to start by contacting a newspaper editor because they're department heads. Like a news director at a TV station, their duties tend to be more executive than editorial.

Joan Stewart, a former newspaper editor herself, says "Editor Sally Smith is probably tied up arguing with the publisher about budgets. She probably has nine performance reviews due by the end of the day and she doesn't have time to hear pitches.

Generally, you'll do much better sending a release or a pitch letter to reporters and columnists.

Reporter and Columnists

These are the lifeblood of almost any print publication. Sometimes, they write about people or topics that are assigned to them. Sometimes they "enterprise" a story, meaning they develop a topic or idea themselves. Therefore, they're the "exceptions" we mentioned above, because they often have a little more license to choose what they want to write about.

If you want publicity from a reporter or columnist though, it's best to send a pitch letter. It's definitely more effective.

Evening TV News

Assignment Editor

Compare the assignment editor of a TV newsroom to a hockey goalie who's trying to watch fifteen players and three pucks coming down ice at him all at once. (OK, this doesn't happen in hockey, but if it did the goalie would understand what the assignment editor is up against on a daily basis).

The assignment editor generally sits behind a huge desk, somewhere near a bank of police, fire, and emergency scanners which he or she listens to at all times.

The assignment editor also receives dozens (some in bigger cities even get hundreds) of news releases, faxes, email and phone calls from people requesting coverage.

He or she also decides which stories will be covered by which reporter or photographer crews, coordinates their movements, handles equipment and vehicle malfunctions, and listens to whining staffers complaining that they missed lunch because of breaking news.

We're not trying to get you to feel sorry for assignment editors, but you do need to understand their state of mind—which is generally just short of frenzy.

Unless you've developed a personal or professional relationship with a reporter or anchor (more on that later), the assignment editor is *the* person you need to know to have any chance of getting airtime during an evening newscast.

Producer
While the assignment editor decides which stories get covered, the producer decides which stories get on the air, and for how long.

The producer is the person who puts together a newscast, or a segment of a newscast. He or she decides how much airtime each story will get, writes some or all of the copy that the anchors read, and physically keeps track of time while the show is in progress on the air.

While producers have a great deal of say about whether a story makes it into a newscast or not, you won't have much contact with them.

If you saw the movie "Broadcast News," you might remember the Holly Hunter role. She was a producer.

There are also *associate producers* who help with newscast production.

Executive Producer
This position goes by different names in different places—it might be called the assistant news director or something else.

Basically, this person is second-in-command in the newsroom, overseeing day-to-day operations and also performing some executive or administrative duties.

As a coverage-seeker, you normally won't have much contact with the executive producer. But since the "E-P" often presides over daily meetings where decisions are made about coverage priorities, he or she can have an impact on your success or lack of it.

News Director or News Manager

This is the department head, and like department heads in just about any company, they spend most of their time budgeting, hiring, firing, negotiating salaries and doing other generic executive duties.

There's very little reason for you to get to know the news director. In fact, any attempt to go through the news director (instead of the assignment editor) to get a story on the air can result in hard feelings and a definite lack of success far into the future.

Anchors

Having a local TV anchor championing a cause for you can be a powerful tool for getting free publicity. But just sending a letter to one asking for their station to come out and cover an event will probably be counter productive.

News anchors tend to get a lot of mail (some of which is unkind and extremely unpleasant), and your letter might sit on the desk for days before anyone gets around to reading it. In fact, it may never be read at all.

Bottom line: unless you already have a personal relationship with a high profile newsperson, don't start your publicity campaign by contacting them.

However, there are other people at TV stations, radio stations, and newspapers who would be happy to hear from you.

Reporters

God bless reporters. They don't make much money, they don't get much of the glory, and they generally work long hours under withering deadline pressure.

But here's the most important thing to remember about reporters if you want to get free publicity.

Very often, they're responsible for coming up with their own story ideas. This is called "enterprising."

"One of the things I used to look for when I was hiring reporters," says former TV news exec Frank Guerra, "was their ability to enterprise."

This is where you can become the reporter's best friend—and get a bonanza of free publicity for yourself.

For the sake of convenience, we'll group newspaper columnists with reporters in this discussion (this may bother some columnists but we hope they'll forgive us).

We'll also group print reporters with broadcast reporters (this will *really* bother some print reporters, but we hope they'll also forgive us).

We're going to talk about anyone who loosely fits the description of "beat" reporter. Anyone who's responsible for staying current with, and reporting on, a certain topic like technology, business, crime, government, health, travel, consumer affairs, etc.

And let's not forget the real heroes of everyday journalism: the general assignment reporters and feature reporters.

While everyone we just mentioned sometimes gets assigned to cover certain stories, very often they find themselves responsible for coming up with their own ideas. This is where your opportunity lies.

For an in-depth discussion of how to "work" reporters, see Joan Stewart's *Special Report #7: How to Write the Perfect Pitch Letter that Convinces an Editor to Write About You*, and *Special Report #25: How to Pitch Reporters Over the Telephone* and Make Every Second Count. Both reports are available through Joan's website at www.get-free-publicity.com/publicityhound.html

TV Morning News, Talk Shows, and Magazine Shows

The decision-making hierarchy for these shows tends to differ somewhat from evening news programs.

Producer

The producer plays more of an important role, often combining "producer duties" and "assignment editor duties."

For example, if you wanted to get coverage on any of these programs, you'd probably be better off writing directly to the producer.

Like the assignment editor, their job is to find interesting stories and interesting guests, and then prepare both the guest and the host for their on-air meeting.

The producer also "screens" guests to make sure they'll be engaging on the air. Whenever you have a conversation with a talk show producer about a possible appearance, remember: *you're being auditioned.* Talk to the producer the way you'd talk to the viewing audience during an appearance. Never, never, *never* brush off a producer thinking you'll save your most charismatic moments for the host.

If you underestimate or minimize the role of the producer, you'll never find yourself sitting across the table from the host.

Host

The host's role varies from station to station, and from host to host.

Some hosts are mainly interested in looking good and sounding smart, but they don't really take much of an active role in selecting guests or planning the show.

Others want total control.

Your best bet in one of these "softer" programs is to start with the producer and then try to build a relationship with both the producer and the host.

How to Get Your Own TV Talk Show

Okay, you say you'd like to use TV to promote yourself, but you're not quite ready for *Oprah, Larry King Live* or *The Today Show* just yet?

Fortunately there are hundreds of smaller TV opportunities available for you to develop your presence, hone your on-air skills, and decrease your nervousness around cameras.

A lot of local cable companies offer a "community TV" channel. In many places they're open to program ideas and suggestions from local people.

At best, you can wind up with your own show, with you as host and interviewer.

At worst, you can offer yourself as a guest to people who already have these shows.

Either way, you'll be amazed how often you hear your local customers and prospects starting to say, "Hey, I saw you on TV the other night while I was channel surfing…"

It's also a great way to sharpen your skills for the day when you land that coveted spot on one of the "biggies."

If you don't already know who your cable provider is, you can call the Alliance for Community Media at 202-393-2650 and ask. Then call the cable station or operator and simply ask who's in charge of community programming. You might also ask for the station's public relations or community affairs director.

You may run into some resistance at first, depending on where you live. In big cities, competition for any amount of airtime can be fierce. But if you persevere, you can usually succeed.

Radio

In big city radio news operations, the job descriptions roughly parallel the TV job descriptions.

Talk show producer

In general, this person's job is much like that of the TV talk or magazine show producer.

He or she will look for topics that are timely and interesting, research them, find engaging guests or experts to discuss them, set interview schedules, confirm interviews, and finally, make sure the guest is in the studio or on the line at air time.

He or she will also sort through mail, email, faxes, and phone pitches, and decide what to toss, what to put away for future reference, and what to put in the line-up for airing in the next few days.

The producer usually also provides background material and even possibly a list of suggested topics or questions for the host.

Once again, the producer is the one who auditions prospective guests — although most of the time, prospective guests don't realize they're being auditioned. From the first moment you're talking to a producer on the phone, that producer is evaluating you for subject knowledge and communications skills.

Host

At many radio stations, especially those located in smaller cities, the host and the producer are the same person. Again, it's generally easy to find this out by calling the switchboard and simply asking.

Hosts have different styles. Some may want to talk to you by phone before a day or so before airtime. Others don't want to talk to you at all until you're in the studio.

Call screener

If the show offers live phone in questions, there will also be a call screener who answers the phones, asks the caller what subject they'd like to discuss, and makes a quick judgment on who to put on the air next.

The screener generally sits in a separate room next to the studio, and is visible to the host through a large window. The screener communicates with the host in a number of different ways: via a computer screen, or by writing on a "slate" and holding it up for the host to see.

Sometimes the producer doubles as call screener. Sometimes, in smaller markets, the host answers the phones "cold" without a screener—but this is extremely rare.

If you've never been on a particular program before, the producer is really the key contact and the person you should start to build up a relationship with.

However, producers change jobs much more often than hosts, so in the long run, you should really work hard on making yourself useful to the host. Ultimately, it's their show—and while a producer does a lot of the "grunt" work, the host has a lot of say.

If the host likes you, you'll get a lot of airtime.

Big Shows, Big Payoffs

If you don't have much experience talking on the air, you'd do well to stick to focus some attention on sharpening your presentation skills on stations in smaller cities.

But if you're already pretty good on the air, you'll get the best return on your investment of time and effort by shooting for shows in bigger cities.

This is a lesson that Alex Carroll and Bart Baggett learned the hard way.

Alex has written several books on excuses people use to avoid traffic citations. Bart is one of the world's top handwriting experts.

Recently they shared some of their radio success stories with us. We were especially interested in how Alex once made two thousand dollars a minute as a guest on one radio show.

My mentor was a guy named Dan Poynter. You may know him—he wrote a book called The Self-Publishing Manual. I asked him how I could sell a book once I wrote it, and he said 'I think you'd do really well promoting it on radio shows.' And I said, 'Well, great, how do I do that?'

He suggested putting an ad in Radio and Television Interview Report. It's this magazine that you can put an ad in, and then it gets mailed out to five or six thousand producers every couple of weeks, and if they like your story, they'll call you up and have you as a guest on their show.

So I did, and I did very, very well from that ad. I got a total of fifty radio interviews out of it. That's far more than most people get, but part of the reason was they stuck me on the front cover because they liked my topic so much. Most people don't get fifty interviews, though. Most people get seven to fifteen, and I learned a couple of things from it that were very, very important.

After I finished doing all fifty of those interviews, I looked at my sales figures, and forty-seven of those shows had yielded three orders or less. Back then we didn't have the Internet, so that came from just giving out my toll-free number at the end of the interview.

However, three of the shows yielded more than two hundred orders each.

So I made more money on those three shows than all those other forty-seven combined. That's when the light bulb went on. That's when I realized 'OK, I'm no rocket scientist, but I'll be those were big shows.' And sure enough, I was right.

The first one I hit it big on was WMJI in Cleveland. I got over two hundred orders on that show. It was the very first show that I hit it big on. And up until that point, I was getting a little discouraged. I began wondering if there was something wrong with me or I wasn't saying the right things.

The problem was that I was doing interviews on small stations out in the middle of nowhere that didn't have any listeners.

So here's what I learned. I went back to the guys who published the Radio Television Interview Report and I said, 'Hey, I just want to do big shows. Do you guys have a database that tells me which ones are the biggest?' They said, 'Yeah, we've got this Publicity Book database that costs $350 bucks.' I told them to mortgage my last credit card and send it to me.

So I got the thing, and I went through it and I spent a couple of weeks trying to figure it out, and I found out that they rank stations in two ways.

Number one, they give you the station's market ranking. And number two, they tell you the station's wattage. Now, you're supposed to be able to tell how big a station is by these two factors. Problem is you can't and here's why.

Because if you look at a station's market ranking, all it does is tell you the size of the city the station broadcasts in.

For example, New York is the biggest radio market in the country. WABC, which is the biggest talk station in the country, has the same market ranking as New York's polka station — which doesn't have enough listeners to fill your garage. So there's a problem there. Market rankings don't actually tell you how many people listen to a station.

So I had to throw that one out. It didn't work for me.

Then I went to the station's wattage. And what I found out disturbed me as well. Because what happens is, in these big markets — New York, Chicago, Dallas, LA, Houston, Philadelphia, San Francisco, whatever — there is so much competition, there are so many stations on the dial, that the FCC can't give out very much wattage, because they'll overlap their signals. So what you have is huge stations with very small wattage. For example, WKTU in New York City has three million listeners, and it only has three thousand watts. People jump up and down about one hundred thousand watt stations, and fifty thousand watt stations — there are thousands of those and they're all across the country — but they're out in the prairies and the mountains. They need that much wattage so they can pull in a few farmers and ranchers.

So very often, the wattage is inversely proportional to the number of the listeners that they have. Because you'll have huge stations in New York and LA that will have a little tiny transmitter, and they have twenty million listeners within fifteen miles of it.

So once I figured that out, I went to work and I said 'Okay, who rates radio stations? Who will tell me how many listeners they actually have?'

I found out there's a company called Arbitron that's very similar to Nielsen for television, and it took me a couple of weeks and a couple of dozen phone calls, and I still don't know how I did it to this day, but I got the vice-president of Arbitron on the phone.

So I just basically told him 'I have a book on how to beat speeding tickets and I have all these small shows calling me but I just want to do the big shows because that's where the money's at. I understand you guys do the ratings. Is there anything you can do to help me?'

Well, he went on to explain to me that they rate 256 markets across the country and they charge fifteen-to-twenty thousand dollars per station per quarter for these ratings. Well, I couldn't afford that (laughs).

So we came to the end of our conversation and I said to him, 'Look is there anything you can do to help me?'

He said, 'Look Alex, I like you and I like your book. Why don't you send me a dozen copies of your book and I'll send you one of our copies from our last ratings book, which is three months old, for the entire country.'

Well, I about fell off my chair. It was the turning point in my life. I got it about four days later. It's the size of a telephone book, and I went through it and I picked out every station in the country with one hundred thousand listeners or more. I built my own database, and I put together a press kit and I started calling these shows, and pitching them, and telling them, 'Hey I'm a great guest, I can be on your show and tell your listeners how to get out of their speeding tickets.

And they were all booking me. And I'd go on their show and instead of selling two or three books, I was selling two or three hundred books. You know, I'd work for ten minutes, I'd go on a morning show and I'd sell, two, three, four, five hundred books. For instance I'd get up at 5:30 in the morning because I live on the West Coast and I'd do a 7:30 interview in Chicago and I'd roll over and go back to sleep and by lunch time I had ten thousand dollars in my bank account.

So that's the secret behind it. It's really about getting on the big shows.

Now there are lots of other secrets involved in it too, but just to give you an idea... to date, just to give you a barometer of where I've progressed with this. I've done well over twelve hundred radio shows, and I've sold a million-and-a-half dollars of my little speeding ticket book, and basically I've been given four-and-a-half million dollars worth of free advertising.

Bart Baggett once got more than two thousand e-zine subscriptions in one hour through a radio appearance. Here's how he did it, in his own words.

I think that's probably the strongest example of using radio to get people to sign up for your newsletter. In fact, based on that event, I really changed my model of doing radio publicity. And it's a little harder to calculate you know, because of when I was doing it, back in '91.

In 1991, I started doing radio interviews—and this is all pre-Internet. And so the way to make money from that is to send books to the bookstores. I absolutely went broke. I ran up the credit cards—it's just an impossible business for a self-publisher because you usually have to have 20 books in every bookstore, and then you have to get motivated to go to the bookstore, and if you have some type of lecture, you have basically a one-time shot.

I mean all these variables making people go and buy things were very hard to predict, so it was a model that was just filled with incredible struggle.

So I thought I would just take the direct marketing approach. I would give out my 1-800 number and I would either have my assistant take the phone calls or, when I got better, I would then actually have a service take the phone calls. And that worked really well for a while and then eventually it sort of burned out. People stopped buying right off the radio when the Internet came along. It's like they just knew that they could probably go online, check you out thoroughly, and then make a more educated buying decision.

It wasn't just me. I noticed it happened across the board with all my other friends who were making full-time livings as radio guests. There were about 10 or 15 of us that went around the country and did speed-reading or memory courses or handwriting analysis courses or similar programs and it was the same story with everyone.

It's like we stopped making as much money as we used to. That was about '99 or 2000. And so, you know, even though I was still doing radio, instead of $8000 in sales off of an 800-number, I was making $3000. Or instead of $1000, I would be making $300. It was really disappointing, considering that it was my main revenue source.

But as I began focusing on the Internet, my Internet revenue began to match, or in some cases exceed, the direct response revenue. Which was, of course, good news for me.

And so I figured, if this is true, if the Internet is going to keep outpacing this other revenue, then maybe I could just depend on that. And I started using the radio for lead-generation only.

Now lead-generation is different from revenue generation, because you put 300 people on your newsletter list, but you don't make money on them right away. In the 'old' days, I could measure how much each radio appearance generated in sales. With lead generation, you don't always make money right away. You just get names into your database.

But now I can track somebody and I can also track how much that person buys over the next 6 months.

And what I'm finding is the average radio station that back in '94 was worth $3000, in '99 was worth $300 because I wasn't capturing leads and wasn't getting any sales.

Now, though, it's back up to $2000 or $3000, because every one of those leads gets my newsletter, and eventually, a lot of them wind up buying something from me. Some end up spending $1000.

So now it's more viable because I can tap those leads. With my mailing lists up to 60,000 subscribers now and the different areas I'm in, I'm finding now I can make more money off those shows, which for a while I couldn't.

As for the day I got two thousand subscribers in one hour, here's how that happened.

During my radio appearances, I tell the listeners I'm going to give away a copy of my latest book.

And happens is the radio host is going to promote it for me, because I'm giving away something for free, with real tangible value, on the show. That's the key. But, it has to be done a certain way.

See, normally, they're not going to promote your product for you. But here's what I did with a station in Denver that resulted in the 2000 subscribers.

The station I appeared on in Denver calls itself Power 106. I used that to create a sense of urgency among listeners by saying I was going to give a free book to the first 106 listeners to go to the website and sign up for my newsletter.

This is an important piece of information, because if you don't do this, you're basically saying anyone can have the book for free, which then removes all sense of urgency. They think anyone can download this book for free.

Obviously, I'm not going to ship a hard copy to them, but they going to get the whole book on a PDF file. And you know, that was confusing two years ago, but it's not as confusing now. I mean these people understand that we're not going to ship them the book for free. They understand that when they go to the website and subscribe, they can download an electronic version of the book.

This show was a very high rated show and we basically said we'd give away free books to the first 106, but I knew—and they knew—we really wouldn't limit it to the first 106. Be-

cause you're not going to stop, you're not going to say, 'I'm sorry, 107th person, but you can't have it.'

Because they don't really want to leave anyone out, but they also know that saying 'the first 106' it makes it sound special. Radio stations all have in particular attachments or call letters. So giving away $106 or 106 books actually makes them seem special because we're doing something just for their listeners.

And the really nice thing is that you're customizing it for their listeners only, which then causes goodwill for the station. If the listeners like the book, they appreciate the station for helping them get it for free.

You know, that's why they do giveaways and you know it all goes back to ratings.

But Bart is quick to point out that this system only works if you have other products you can sell later to the people who got the free copies. That's called the "backend."

Now this model only works if you have a strong back end. If you only have one book, then you can't give away your one book to build a mailing list. I mean you could, but it would be better to create a special report and give that away and then hopefully those will up-sell your book.

You know, I probably could have sold 30 books on the show, right? Or 30 courses or whatever. But instead I got about 2000 subscribers who then became prospects for all my products. You do the math. If every one of those subscribers has a potential of spending $1000, then you have a prospective pool of customers that can spend $30,000 or $100,000.

I've always found that building mailing lists and building relationships leave a much higher closing percentage then getting customers on the first buy.

So to wrap up the Denver story, here's what I did. I said, 'Hey the first 106 callers get a free book and we had 2030 by the end of the day. I tracked them, and by the end of the day I made $250. Well, not impressive. I could have made a lot *more then $250 if I would have sold some books or sold a course right? But over the next 3 months, that same group of people spent almost $4,500. I looked at all the orders from Denver; and sure enough, 3 or 4 of those people spent $1,000. And a lot of spent some money on other things and a lot of these people are buying stuff today from that show nine months ago. They didn't have the money then, but still liked me, and they're buying from me now.*

Radio producers and hosts are happy to give you free publicity as long as you give their audiences — and them — something of value. When you do, they'll invite you back again and again. According to Alex Carroll, it's not hard to understand this "you scratch my back, I'll scratch yours" philosophy.

They only care about one thing: keeping the listeners they have and bringing in more. Because that's what drives their paychecks. When their ratings go up, they can charge more dollars for their advertising, and they're happy. If their ratings go down, they're in trouble. They lose their jobs. So the way they make the ratings go up is to provide good content.

If you have good content, they want you as a guest on their show. If you can save people time or money, if you can make them rich, if you can tell them an amazing story, if you can make them laugh, if you can share little known tips or secrets, if they can teach them something new, if you can get them arguing — because radio people love controversy — it lights up their phones, and they want you on their show.

It's a barter. Basically, you give them great content, you give them a great show, you entertain their listeners, and you inform their listeners. In turn, they give you a plug. That's it. That's the bottom line.

So when you're doing this, it's not about what you're selling... I mean, yeah, you're selling a book, or selling a website, or selling whatever... but that's not what the real focus is. The focus is the show.

You've got to come up with a show. And to the host or the

producer, you're selling them on a show. And THAT'S the critical thing.

In the radio publicity course Alex offers, he spells out four different ways you can get interviews on radio.

Number one—and a lot of people try this—you can send out those mass mailing, mass faxes, and mass email blasts to producers.

Number two, you can hire a PR firm. It can be effective. If you don't have any time and you have lots of money, you can hire a PR firm, and you're going to pay for it—they're going to charge you anywhere from two to ten thousand dollars a month in retainer fees, regardless of how many shows they book you on.

If you're going to hire a PR firm, be sure to hire a good one. They'll have all the connections and they'll plug you in and you'll pay a lot for it but at least you'll get something for your money.

If you hire a lousy PR firm they'll book you on a bunch of dinky little shows in bad time slots, and you will not at all get your money's worth. So be careful with that one.

Number three, you can do what I did in the beginning, which is to advertise in these publications and services which list guests that are available for radio shows.

If you take that approach, I would recommend you do Radio Television Interview Report. It's actually a good thing to start out with because it kind of gives you a chance to get your feet wet, to get your spiel down and get some practice before you go screwing up on bigger stations. Because the majority of producers and hosts that call you from that are smaller. It's not their fault. It's just a numbers game. There are, like eleven thousand radio stations in the country and there are only a few hundred of them that have more than a hundred thousand listeners. So the vast majority of your invitations are going to come from the smaller stations because that's just the way the demographics break down.

The fourth way that you get on radio shows is that you call the shows and you pitch them yourself. And I'll tell you why this works.

First of all, because you are building a personal relationship with a producer or a host. In most cases you're pitching a producer. And for radio people—unlike television or print or any other type of publicity—the most important thing is what you sound like. Because they're going to be talking to you on the air. They want to know how you sound. They want to know if you're articulate and can get to the point, or if you're boring and monotonous and can't get anything said. That's what they want to know.

So when you call them and you talk to them, they get an instant feel for how good you are. If you've got your pitch down and you can get to the point, they're much more likely to book you. So that's why calling the stations and pitching them yourself is a really powerful way to go.

You know when they book some guest through a PR firm and the PR firm always says 'Oh yeah, they're a great guest.' I don't know how many radio people I talk to who say, 'It's a nightmare. We book these guests through PR firms and the guests suck. And we have to hang up on them because they're so bad. We like being able to talk to you because we can tell you're a good guest. We don't have to worry about hanging up on you and filling the time with something else.'

Alex believes that's what makes radio a better "selling medium" than TV.

First of all, when you're on the radio, you get far more time to talk. The average interview on a music station is about fifteen minutes. The average interview on a talk station is a half-hour to an hour. So you get a lot more time, whereas on television they'll tape you for, I don't know, sometimes and hour or even two hours. Then they'll cut it down to three minutes. You have no control over what goes into the broad-cast.

*Another good thing about radio is you don't have to deal
with stage fright. A lot of people really freak out when someone sticks a camera in their face. You don't have to deal with
that in radio at all because almost all your interviews are
done by telephone. They call you wherever you're at. You
don't have to get dressed up. You can be traveling; you can
be on an airplane, or in a hotel.*

*With radio you also get live audience interaction, which you
hardly ever get on television. You get listeners calling in, and
they ask you questions. You give you feedback. You find out
what they like and what they don't like. You add stuff to your
presentation with practically every interview you do because
you get this feedback. You don't get that with print, and you
don't get that with television.*

*Plus you get to give out your contact information. You get
to give out your toll-free number, you get to give out your
website, and you get sales and cash in the bank in forty-
eight hours. You don't get that with television. They tape
those things and air them three months later. With print,
sometimes they have a six-month lead-time. And the print
people... well, sometimes they'll print your website but a lot
of the time they won't.*

*And the final reason I like radio so much better is that it's
just a more powerful medium. Most people are shocked at
this statistic, but it's the most popular medium in the country. Ninety-six percent of the U.S. population listens to radio
every week and seventy-five percent of the population listens
every single day. And when you think about it, it's common
sense, because radio is the only medium that reaches people
in their cars, and virtually everyone drives back and forth to
work every day. And when they're driving back and forth to
work they're listening to radio. And there's no other medium
that has that kind of an audience. It's extremely powerful.*

Radio, though, may be the most demanding medium on a guest. You
have to be able to hold the listener's attention for a longer period of

time, and Alex says you'll always do well if you're passionate about your topic.

Producers are looking for a lot of different things from a guest, but the single most important thing they're looking for is energy. They want you to be fired up, they want you to be excited, they want you to be articulate, and they want you to have a point to make and something of value to provide to their audience. They want you to be able to hold the audience's interest so they don't change the channel to another station. You need to be able to convey that, to be able to capsulate your show idea.

If you send a press release you've got to make sure it's got a good headline, and some bullet points that will tell them what you're going to share with their audience, and you make it easy for them by creating a list of sample questions so that they can go right down the list of sample questions. Your interview is pre-scripted for them.

You want to make it as easy for them as you possibly can, because the easier you make it for them to book you, the more likely they are to do it. Because they do not have time to do research and dream up questions for you. You just give them a turnkey interview, and they're going to be much more apt to book you.

Here's another important point. Look at it from the perspective of the hosts. They know that if you give them a sample list of questions, aside from the fact that they don't have time to dream up their own anyway, they know that if they stick to those questions, you're going to know the answers.

They want you to sound good. They're having you on the show because they want you to sound good. They don't want you to sound bad. So if they start asking you questions that aren't on your list, they don't know what they're going to get. But they know if they stick to the questions on your list, you're going to sound good.

Alex has done a masterful job of using radio to build a subscriber list.

Like Bart, he knows that the best way to get someone to give you his or her email address is to give him or her something of value first.

What I would do is at the end of my interviews, when I gave out my website, I would say, 'By the way, we give out a free copy of my book every week to the person who gives the best ticket story or excuse. And you can also get the winning ticket story of the week emailed to you if you just go to my site and punch in your email address. So I've built a rather sizeable list of subscribers who get the winning speeding excuse every week. And they occasionally get other offers that can turn out to be quite lucrative.

Freebies are really important. I have a free list of speed traps for every state in the country. In fact, I made an arrangement back in 1995 when Andrew Warner was first starting his speedtrap.com website before it got really huge. And I in fact am one of the reasons that site got so huge. I called him up and said, 'Hey Andrew, I'd like to build your site for you, and I'd like to give away a list of your speed traps to everybody who purchases my book, and of course, you'll get a plug out of it.

And he said 'Yeah, of course.'

And it was really great because my sales tripled overnight when I did that. I went from telling people to call toll-free, visit the website and buy the book, to telling people 'If you mention this show when you buy the book you get a free list of speed traps for your state along with the book...' Just like that, I can't tell you how many people will buy whatever it is you're selling to get whatever it is you're giving away for free. It really works.

The thing is, giving away something like lists is really awesome because they have high perceived value, but they have very little cost to you. Duplication costs two or three cents, but the perceived value is enormous.

Ed Taylor of The Internet Marketing Group uses a technique similar to the one Alex described. He told us about it during an interview we did recently for our Internet radio show.

> One of the things that I feel absolutely crucial in the development of and website Internet marketing strategy is the development of what I call a 'pull component.' You need something that will give your target a market a compelling reason to visit your site.

> I do a lot of radio interviews, and I started thinking a few years ago, 'What can I do on a radio program that would cause this target market to visit our site?'

> Here's what I came up with.

> I usually spend most of my interview time going through specifics on what you people can do to optimize their websites for search engines. As we get down to the last few minutes, I normally say something like:

> 'George, thanks so much for having me on your program today. I really, I hope that your listeners are getting some great ideas that they can use immediately to enhance their experience and their success on the Internet. Unfortunately, but we didn't really have time to cover something that I've found to be critically important: the mistakes that people make. I've identified George, what I call the, '10 Fatal Flaws of Internet Marketing.' These are mistakes that anyone who's listening right now just cannot afford to make. Any one of these mistakes will doom you to fail on the Internet and unfortunately today, we don't have time to cover that.'

> Of course, the interviewer is going to ask, 'Well, is there a place where our listeners can get the information?'

> And I say,

> 'As a matter of fact there is. I've created this free report at our website that any of your listeners can access instantly. All they have to do is go to www.internetmarketinggroup.com. There's a big display ad on there that says the 10 Fatal Flaws

of Internet Marketers. Fill out a brief form and get the free report.'

You see this sort of a "pull" every night on your evening news. The anchors will try to hook your attention with an intriguing detail about an upcoming story—just before going to a commercial. In the news business, these brief snippets are called "teases."

Ed suggests you can even use pull components in your other advertising.

Think about this. What if I were to offer a free report in my yellow page ad? 'The Ten Most Common Mistakes People Make When Having Their Website Developed.' It helps pull people to my website to get that free white paper.

Don't just give people your URL. Give them a reason to visit. A pull.

For anyone who's serious about getting free publicity on radio, Alex Carroll's eighteen hour "Radio Publicity Masters Course" is an absolute must.

As part of the program, he actually lets you listen in as he talks to radio producers on the phone.

In one recent month, he booked seventy-seven interviews, which directly resulted in more than $50,000 in sales.

To visit his "Radio Publicity" website, go to www.get-free-publicity.com/radiopublicity.html

When you sign up for his newsletter, you'll also get a free list of the Top 20 Nationally Syndicated Radio Talk Shows, complete with addresses, phone numbers and names of both the hosts & the producers! Together, these shows reach 75 million people!

Bart Baggett offers a number of websites on a number of topics. Besides his expertise in handwriting analysis, he's also published several works on the topic of success.

You can reach Bart at www.get-free-publicxity.com/bartbaggett.html

How to Get Your Own Radio Show

If you like the idea of being a regular guest on radio shows, how would you like the idea of hosting your own?

You don't need *any* experience, you don't need a journalism degree, and you don't need any special training.

All the really need is the courage to do it, and the willingness to muddle through some understandable nervousness while you get comfortable around microphones.

Everybody who has never done radio before gets stage fright at first.

But after a while, you get over it. In fact, you begin to love being on the air. Radio is, by far, the world's most user-friendly offline medium.

And by the way, you can even make money, get lots of free stuff, and go to concerts, sports events, fund raising galas and other things most people have to pay for—without spending a dime for any of it.

You might also build your opt-in list enormously.

So what's the secret? How do you get invited to do your own show?

You don't wait to get invited. You create a show of your own by finding sponsors who will back you. Then you approach radio stations and buy 30-60 minutes of airtime from them.

Dozens of entrepreneurs around the USA are doing it, and Mike Litman is among the most successful.

He shared his story with us recently during a break from his emcee duties at Mark Joyner's "Survival Tactics for Tough Times" seminar in Los Angeles.

> My parents lived on Long Island near a tiny radio station half the size of your kitchen table. The signal is so weak you might not hear it a couple of blocks away.
>
> Well, one day I was invited to be a guest, and I really enjoyed it. I started wondering how I could get a show of my own?
>
> There was only one option open to me: buying the time. I

*literally bought ad time on a radio show in Long Island; I was
24 years old then. I started interviewing my celebrities. Not
Brad Pitt or Jennifer Aniston, but my celebrities—Mark Vic-
tor Hansen, Famous Amos, and Michael Gerber and all these
great personal development experts. I've been reading about
these and reading their books reading their books till 3:00
o'clock in the morning when I was going to sleep.*

*For nine months I interview these people. I don't think I ever
had more than 3 people listening live: my parents and this
guy named Jason Oman who was in California, 3,000 miles
away. He actually used to call the station and listen to the
show on the phone while he was on hold.*

*So this was 1998. I did it for nine months and had trouble
making any money with it. So I moved out of my home, got
a job in New York City. Then another job. I had three jobs in
three years.*

*By now it was February of 2001. I got a call from 3,000 miles
away. It was Jason in California.*

*He said, 'Mike you know those radio show tapes from when
you did that show 3 years ago?'*

*And I said I haven't seen them in three years. They were in a
box at my parents' house gathering dust.*

*He says 'Let's get them transcribed and turn them into a
book called, 'Conversations with Millionaires.'*

*We shopped the idea with some publishers, and they all said
that nobody would read conversations. So we self-published.*

*Seventy-six days later the book hit number one on Amazon's
'Big List.'*

*It's now been translated in 3 languages. And it all happened
because I followed my dream and pursued my own radio
show.*

By the way, Mike is back on the air at the same station. It's still "half
the size of your kitchen table," but Mike says he found out that it
doesn't matter.

He also found out that it doesn't matter how many people are listening, or what the ratings are. You can still attract incredibly qualified, high profile people to come on your show. We asked Mike how he was able to do that.

> That's the question people ask me more often than any other.
>
> The bottom line is you need to ask for what you want. I just called these people up and asked. But here's the real key.
>
> Remember, these are people that I've always admired. I always showed them that I was familiar with their material, that I had read their books. I 'd tell them 'I've been through this and this and ask them a question about it. They say 'Wow, this guy is for real.' So being prepared was really important for my credibility. Get some information, do some research, and you can connect with people intimately. When you do, you'll see great things happen.
>
> I didn't need to tell these people I only have ten listeners. You just tell them the truth. You have a radio show on personal development. It fits their market. They easily could have said no. They could have easily asked how many people tune in and what are your ratings, all that kind of stuff. But they never did.

Mike has now packaged his knowledge into an audio cassette series which he sells at his website www.mikelitman.com

One of his first buyers was Mark Crowley of Denver. He took the strategies and techniques he learned in Mike's course and parlayed it into his own show on Denver station KNUS, AM 710. He says

> I was introduced to Mike and we began corresponding by email quite a bit. I began to notice that Mike was promoting information products through his radio show, including a set of tapes that tells you how to get a show of your own. 'So I bought it.
>
> It took me about 10 days to listen to it, and when I was through, I decided to do it.

I came up with a concept and took it went looking for an opportunity to buy time for the show. That's what they call a broker relationship.

The next big step was to find a way to pitch the concept to a station. Though a mutual friend, I was able to visit with the station manager at KNUS and he said he liked the concept. He asked me to put together a formal proposal and then come back.

I found out later he didn't really expect to see me again, because ninety-nine out of a hundred people don't follow through. But I did. So we sat down, hammered it out, actually created the show and got on the air.

I really didn't have any radio background at the time, except for a short stint as a part time deejay at a tiny, low wattage station back in the early 80's. But when you move from spinning records to modern day digital talk radio it's two different worlds. So really, I feel comfortable in saying I had no experience.

Mark doesn't rely on income he generates from product promotion to pay for the show. He went out and recruited sponsors to help defray the expense of buying the time.

I operated just as any other radio program would. A lot of brokered shows are really infomercials. But I decided that I wanted to stay with the format of the radio station and look like I was 'part of the family.' But I actually go out and sell my spots just like the sales department at the station.

Sponsorship on a radio show of our nature is very unique because most advertisers depend on repetition in order to achieve their goal. Well we're on for an hour once a week, so we've really focused on image. We have a successful image and the sponsors want to be associated with that image. Our biggest sponsor is Ford Dealership in Denver, and when I brought the concept to them they didn't even hesitate because they wanted to be associated with that image. They knew the show was going to go someplace, so they came right onboard.

We asked Mark what gave him the confidence to go out and say, "Hey, I can do this."

It was Mike Litman's audio series. He put everything in very simple terms. He really laid it out and here's the step to go through and most importantly he told in that series what the possibilities were and how that the radio stations can truly become a vehicle to market whatever it is that you're trying to market. In my case it was seminars regarding achievement and that since have evolved to some other things.

Mike helped me understand how I could use a radio show as a medium to market my products and myself in a very incredible way.

The show has benefited me in many, many ways.

First of all, I got my name out in the radio marketplace, and that helped boost my credibility. People want to be associated with anyone in the media. So I find that people are now coming to me asking me to be on my show, rather me having to go out and ask them.

And of course, Mark is using the show as a vehicle for building his newsletter subscriber base.

We built a website that operates behind the radio show and we're doing just the things that you need to do. We're building a list, we have a newsletter that comes out once a week, we have a daily power course that goes out everyday, six days a week and through our subscription service.

We're finding that people who opt into our newsletter list are hungry for more information and they're looking for what we offer.

Don't get the impression though, that everything automatically falls into place, and it's easy because he's only on for an hour each week.

It's definitely work. I spend a great number of hours planning each show. When you hear the end product on the radio, it sounds great, looks like it might be easy, but it's not easy. Simple but not easy—they're two different things.

It's not difficult though, Mark says, to find guests.

They come from everywhere. I subscribe to a magazine called RTIR. It stands for 'Radio, Television Interview Report.' I got some from there in the beginning. But now I'm going to a lot of seminars and live events, meeting people who are authors and have information products. All those people realize how much radio helps them get the word out. So now I have people coming to me wanting to be on the show.

Some people are intimidated by the technology they see in the studio.

There's a lot of it. In fact it looks like the control center on the Starship Enterprise from Star Trek.

But a lot of it is automation. Plus, the station provides an engineer who runs the computers, opens the microphones, screens my callers, and so on. All I have to do is make sure that every single week I come in with quality products to put out to my listeners.

Check out Mark Crowley's website at www.successradioshow.com, and when you're in the Denver area, listen to his show, every Sunday at noon Mountain Time USA.

Chapter 4
How to Approach Media Decision-Makers

The most powerful and productive way to generate free publicity is through long-term, professional relationships with media decision-makers.

But even a novice with no journalism background or public relations experience can get an amazing amount of media coverage with a well-written press release. The press release is the single most important—and to most people, the most mysterious—vehicle for attracting positive attention from the media.

Big city news operations receive hundreds of news releases a day. Only a small percentage ever gets into the hands of a reporter, producer, or columnist. Even fewer result in coverage.

Why?

Well, sheer volume is the most obvious cause. To paraphrase a popular bumper sticker, "So many news releases, so little time".

But actually, there are a number of other reasons, and they're just as important:

- They're cumbersome to read because of poor formatting, small print, etc.
- They're blatant attempts to promote a person or a product
- They're not about newsworthy subjects
- They're not suited to the medium they're sent to
- They're too long—journalists are too pressed-for-time to read them

Most press releases fall into one of the categories above. Only 5-10 percent get more than a quick glance. A few seconds and that's it.

Do you have to be some kind of PR genius—or at least a very good writer—to create an effective press release?

Do you have to spend hours meticulously working and reworking your copy so it grabs the attention and interest of editors, producers and reporters?

Do you need to spend a bundle on a pricey agency that will distribute your release to thousands of media contacts for you?

Absolutely not.

But you do have to know a couple of basics that, fortunately, are not that hard to learn.

We recently gathered three veteran journalists for a discussion about press releases.

The panelists included:

Frank Guerra

Frank worked as a reporter, assignment editor and news executive at KENS TV in San Antonio, Texas for nearly fifteen years. In 1995 he co-founded the marketing and media firm of Guerra, DeBerry, and Coody. Frank has "worked both sides of the street," as he puts it: as a journalist responsible for making decisions about what stories got on the air, and as a public relations executive trying to get free publicity and news coverage for his clients. During his career, Frank has read, literally, thousands of press releases.

Joan Stewart

Joan is a former newspaper reporter and editor with more than twenty years experience in the print media. She is the former editor of the Milwaukee Business Journal.

Pat Rodgers

Pat says he's been in radio for so long that "all of today's nostalgia tunes were new releases" when he started. Pat has worked as a radio news anchor, reporter and talk show host for more than 35 years.

Most of that time, he was the news director at WOAI, a 50,000-watt, 24-hour news and information station in San Antonio.

Frank Guerra offered the first tip.

First of all, it's got to be clean and simple. When I'm sitting on the desk, imagine what I'm balancing… I've got a reporter on the phone who's telling me a story has basically died, and I've got to find a way to resurrect it because it's got to be the lead at 5:00. I've got the police scanner… I've got a news van that's broken down… I've got the radio going. I don't mean listening to the top 40… I mean listening to the police scanner, the fire scanner, the public safety scanner… the producer is barking in my ear… all of these things going on at once. The phone is ringing off the hook… you really juggle a lot of things at once.

Imagine in that environment you get a press release, a news release, whatever you want to call it, that is just chock-full of information and it looks like a textbook. I will toss that… it will go in the trashcan so quickly because I don't have the time.

The best release that lands on an assignment editor's desk is one that is very simple and very easy to read. It's got to have a good, catchy headline that captures my attention. It's got to tell me who's going to be there, what it's going to be about, some of the visuals that will be supported there… in other words, we're going to have this press conference, but here's some of the visuals that we're also going to have. You might want to put why in there, and you want to put where. Very simple, bulleted information.

You always have to have a contact name and phone number. Make sure it's a phone number that's going to work at the time of the event. A lot of people make the mistake that they send it out on Thursday or Friday for a weekend event and they give the phone number to the office… they're not at the office; they're at the event. So make sure it's a phone number that works on the day and the time of the event.

Also be sure to include a phone number and a contact name if people want to get information in advance.

So those very basic elements in a very clean format... it goes so much further than some dissertation that someone writes. People somehow think it's the other way around... the more I write, the better the chance I'll get coverage. That is not the case.

Most people tend to give "TMI" when writing a press release: "Too Much Information." They include details about irrelevant facts, and often they try to impress the decision-maker by dumping in a lot of unnecessary background or biological information. Frank says those things tend to be counterproductive.

What really makes a good press release is a headline that captures my attention... something that just stands out, and I think... oh, that's interesting...I've got to read a little bit further.

And then very bulleted information: what is the event, who is going to be there, when is it going to be... be sure you give the specific time, and where... with very specific instructions if it's a difficult place to get to. You also need to be sure you include contact name and numbers. Make sure it's information that's relevant on the day that you're having the event.

So many times I would get a press release on a Wednesday or a Thursday for a weekend event, but they would give a phone number that didn't work. It was ringing at the guy's office while he was out at the ballpark. And, finally, be sure to offer information about visuals that are available. That will really capture the attention of a TV news assignment editor.

Joan Stewart says that during her career as a reporter and editor, she often heard from people who agonized over the wording and the format of a press release. For instance, she says, some people tell you that a release must always be a single page, double-spaced.

I'm going to say something that a lot of publicists might dis-agree with, and something that might be very surprising to people. I think there is so much attention, and worry, and sweat, and bloodshed over how the news release needs to be written. People spend hours on these things, and they don't need to.

So you don't need to sweat bullets over the wording of the news releases. If you can tell the media up front clearly, concisely, and quickly, what the event is, where it's being held, what time and most importantly, why their readers should care... they'll pick up on it.

If you sent the same release to eight different newspapers, that release would be written eight different ways.

This is really important. Write a news release for five different media outlets in your community. Send that release to each outlet, accompanied by a cover letter that suggests a specific angle or somebody interesting that they might want to cover. Make those cover letters different for each of those five media outlets. Let each of them get something a little bit different about the story, so they all don't end up with the same story. You know, the media hate that.

Over the years, Pat Rodgers has seen thousands of press releases. While he says he agrees that "simple is better," there have been times when publicity-seekers have gotten his attention by getting a little bit creative.

The most effective attention-getter for me came from a software company. The software was supposed to teach you about your anatomy. Instead of just sending a press release, they sent me an actual x-ray in a large envelope. On it they had their logo and in it they had a short press release, telling me a) what the program was about, and b) how to get hold of them. And that's all I wanted to know anyway. Guess who got on the air? Because it stuck out in the stack. It was simple. It was clever. I thought it should be rewarded... and it met my needs, obviously.

You want to catch their attention with something that has a little bit of imagination. If you can, be creative about what you send... that thing that gets into the hands of the produc-

er, the thing that gets into the hands of the talk show host... whatever it might be. If it's clever enough and has a connection with what it is you're about to talk about, it really does make a difference in whether or not I'll go to the next stage to see what this is all about.

You have to realize that we're working always under a tight schedule. When I get that piece of mail or that fax... or now an email, I'm only going to look at the first paragraph. If you haven't interested me in the headline or the first paragraph or two, if I don't understand what it is you want from me and who you are, and what you can give me—not necessarily in that order—I may not pay attention. If you bury that information on page 2 or somewhere down at the bottom of the page, I'm never going to figure out who you are. So give me the basics—the who, what, when, where, and why kind of thing. If you can do it in bullet point to start with, that's even better. I look at a page and you have twenty seconds to distill who you are and what you have and whether I want you.

Do You Have to Be a PR Pro to Get Results With a Press Release?

Remember David Frey and MakeTheGrade.com? David has become pretty proficient at using press releases to promote his businesses and consulting practices.

He's a marketing expert, but he has no formal training in writing or creating releases. Nonetheless, he distributes them regularly, and with considerable success.

David had great success with MakeTheGrade.com, but his strategy, he says, can be used in just about any small business.

Let me give you some different examples... Let's suppose that you're an accountant, and as accountant you developed a press release about tax planning, and maybe you gave some tax planning tips.

Well as an accountant, you could offer a list of tax planning dos and don'ts... Maybe you could put the top 15 dos and don'ts of tax planning in an auto responder.

If you're restaurant and you're targeted to the healthy food eaters, you can offer a list of healthy foods, the calorie counts of those foods, or a list of rules for eating in a healthy way. Those are some different things that you can do for a restaurant.

Now suppose you ran an auto repair shop... You could do a press release that talked about many of the ways that auto repair shops scam unsuspecting consumers. Or you could write a press release about how to keep your car in running order and you could offer a checklist of the items that they would need to check on a periodic basis on the car. You could even give them how many miles that need to be checked. And that's a nice little simple checklist that any auto repairs shop that ought to be able to provide that the consumer would be interested in responding to.

I live in south Texas, and when we get a lot of rain there are cars that sometimes go through those low water crossings... and they become damaged. Then people try to sell the cars after that because they start having all sorts of problems with them.

So I went to this particular auto repair shop and said 'Can you give me a list of 4 or 5 tips that somebody who's buying a used car could look for so that they would be able to tell if the car has some water damage of some kind?'

Well, I can tell you that topic got a lot of play here in Houston when the floods came through, because a lot of the auto dealers were reselling these cars that had gotten flooded to unsuspecting victims.

David made a key point that has been mentioned before, but it bears repeating.

When you prepare a press release, it's important to remember that you're not trying to tell the whole story in the release itself. You're just trying to get the media decision-maker's interest, and to motivate them to contact you to learn more (or even do a story).

David has enjoyed a lot of free publicity because he understands how the game is played, and what hooks a decision-maker's attention.

He offers some further examples small businesses can use.

First, create a press release and then create an easy checklist. Do it in a text file and then offer that text file in an auto responder and you'll be able to capture a lot of email addresses.

Now when I did my press release for www.makethegrade.com it went out to 400 lifestyle editors to the biggest magazines. Because I don't subscribe to a clipping service, I don't know how many newspapers published it. However, several people did tell me where they saw it. And the people that did were all the way from Cleveland to Washington down in Florida. So I know it got published in multiple newspapers. And by the way, the traffic to my site just flew and I must have collected probably about 600 email addresses. Just from one press release. For free.

It took me about half a day to develop and about an hour for me to develop my checklist and then shoot it out.

Often-Overlooked Reasons to Distribute a News Release

Excerpted from
The Instant Press Release Toolkit
www.pressreleasetoolkit.com

You don't need to have front-page news to send out a news release.

You don't want to 'spam' journalists with drivel, of course. But you DO want to keep your name, your letterhead, and your logo in front of them.

Don't expect them to do a story every time you send them a release. Your success in getting coverage often depends on a lot of things that are completely out of your control.

There are days when even the most newsworthy events get crowded out by other stories. The important thing is just to keep trying, and if you do, you'll enjoy your share of successes.

Here are some often-overlooked reasons for sending out a release.

- *Accomplishments, awards, and other forms of recognition*
- *Anniversaries and milestones in company history*
- *Appearances by company executives or employees at important community events*
- *Appointments to boards and committees, or formation of boards and committees*
- *Articles by you or about you in publications, or news stories on TV and radio or in print.*
- *Birthdays—yours or those of important people in your organization*
- *Celebrity visits*
- *Charity projects, donations or volunteering by you or company employees*
- *Continuing or community education classes you are teaching, sponsoring or supporting*
- *Contests you're sponsoring or promoting, especially if they're connected to a charity*
- *Controversy (NOTE: taking a stand on a controversial issue can be especially effective if you can become spokesman for an organization that has a position)*
- *Death of an important person in your organization*
- *Fundraisers—including the kickoff, ongoing progress reports, and the conclusion of the effort*
- *Giveaways—free samples, free products or services*
- *Grants, either giving or getting*
- *Holiday celebrations, fundraisers, gifting or community involvement*

- *Interviews or appearances of company executives or employees on TV, radio, print*
- *Mergers, acquisitions or new alliances*
- *New company name or address*
- *New facilities—announcement of, groundbreaking ceremonies, progress reports, opening*
- *New job, career, or situation*
- *New job creation by companies, especially if that position has never existed before*
- *New hours, especially if they're unusual or "groundbreaking" in some way*
- *New website*
- *Newsletter you're starting, especially if it's an electronic newsletter*
- *Open houses and tours of your facilities, plant, etc., especially if they're new*
- *Predictions or forecasts by company officials, researchers, or executives*
- *Printing of your name or a quote of yours in a book or an article*
- *Public Stock Offering*
- *Retirement of key or longtime employees*
- *Speaking engagements*
- *Trade show activity*
- *White paper, position paper, and manuscript someone has written.*
- *Workshops you're presenting or attending*

Press Release Delivery Vehicles: Fax, Email or Mail?

It used to be that news releases were delivered by mail or by hand.

Then along came fax machines. They were cheaper and faster.

Then along came email. Almost instantaneous, and practically cost-free. You can announce your news to thousands of journalists all at once.

But now how do you know you're sending it to someone who's likely to read it and then act upon it?

Dr. Kevin Nunley is a former radio personality who also has a Ph.D. in Communications. After working from a number of radio stations, he discovered the Internet, and started a company that helps writers get their work into publications and media of all kinds.

He's an expert at distributing news releases and articles, and he says there are a number of options to consider when you want to contact journalists.

In our company, we really go two ways. We want to have an in-house list, which we originally purchased from Gebbie Press several years ago. I think Gebbie has about the cheapest but best-quality list out there. It's updated every year and I think it costs about $100.

The problem with almost any list is that a lot of the addresses are going to be dead because you know, as they say in radio, if you don't like who you're working with just wait a month or so and they'll be gone. Somebody will be in his or her place.

There are revolving doors in a lot of places, plus they're constantly bought, sold, etc. There's been a lot of that in the last few years.

We just built up our own house lists after a while, taking people off that didn't want to be on there, and adding people who did.

For about $150 you can have your release sent to every media in your state, which are usually the media who are going to cover you anyway. It also goes to approximately 3,500 online media contacts.

But the other thing I tell people is that, in most cases the press release distribution people do not have an 'in' with any media, but they may have a few friends here and there. For the most part your average editor doesn't know one distribution place from the next.

Now, if you want to hire a publicist, where someone actually pitches your story for you, it's probably going to cost you a lot of money. If you're a small businessperson on a tight budget, you're probably better off having a distribution service send out your release. Then, go back and yourself contact six or seven publications that cover your particular industry.

Some of my customers have done really well with publicity, and that's exactly how they've done it. It's been two-pronged approach, where they send out a mass press release using our service, and then they follow up themselves with selected editors, reporters, and so on.

The Fear Factor

Writing and distributing press releases is like learning to use a computer. At first it scares you because you don't understand how it works, and you don't know what you need to know about using it.

After a while though, you become comfortable with it.

Then after a little while longer, you can get addicted to sending them out because the return on investment is so powerful.

For more detail on the subject of press releases, check out the Instant Press Release Toolkit at www.pressreleasetoolkit.com.

The toolkit includes:

Tool #1: Instant Press Releases

This is a combination textbook and private website that gives you:

- A series of fill-in-the-blanks, ready-to-use press release templates. You simply replace the copy in these templates with details of your own. The basic outline is already in place, along with much of the copy. Included are a request-for-coverage template, a ready-to-use template, and templates for promoting books, companies, authors, events, websites, and products and services.
- A fill-in-the-blanks, ready-to-use headline generator. The headline is the most critical element in any release. This tool

makes it easy for you to put a "grabber" at the top of your release.

- More than a dozen in-depth studies of actual press releases, examined the same way a media decision-maker would look at them.
- A list of 33 often overlooked reasons to send out a news release, and lots more...

Tool #2: Start Spreading the News

This is an e-book and private website that includes:

- Tips on how to avoid the 5 biggest bonehead mistakes almost ALL non-professionals make when they write a press release — doing even one of them can send your release sailing into the trash in seconds.
- 3 critical tests your press release must pass before it has any chance of resulting in coverage by any news organization.
- 28 "hot buttons" you can push with media decision-makers that will get their attention — and respect
- The *one* word you *never* want to use in a press release because it will immediately destroy your credibility and result in an instant "blow off" by any respectable journalist
- How to time your press release so that have the best chance of success in newspaper, TV, and print.

Tool #3: The Media "Hit List" And Resource Center

This tool gives you:

- The media "Hit List," a collection of more than 7,000 media contacts
- Access to a searchable database that will make it easy for you to find radio and TV stations, newspapers, magazines, ad agencies and Internet publishers by name, city, or state.
- Links to companies that write and distribute news releases inexpensively and effectively.
- A list of other authors and products related to press releases and getting free publicity.

Once again, the URL for The Instant Press Release Toolkit is www.pressreleasetoolkit.com

Also see Joan Stewart's *Special Report #8: Media Kits On A Shoestring*, and *Special Report #12: Kick Butt News Releases*, at www.get-free-publicity.com/publicityhound.html

Plus, see Appendix A for a list of other media resources.

Chapter 5

Using the Media to Position Yourself As an Expert

Getting free publicity is easy if you're Tom Cruise or Julia Roberts. All you have to do is show up — anywhere.

But if you don't already have a gaggle of paparazzi following you to the dry cleaners, how do you make that important first impression with a reporter, producer, talk show host or editor?

Well, "publish or perish" has been the rule in the academic world since anyone can remember.

It's not necessarily true that you've got to have a book or audio series to gain credibility with the media, but it absolutely helps. It certainly gives you an advantage over someone who isn't "published."

Producing books and products used to be painstakingly slow and — sometimes — prohibitively expensive.

But then along came computers.

Now you can publish an electronic book as fast as you can write it. You can produce an audiotape series in a matter of hours.

My friend Bart Baggett recorded a six-hour audio series in one weekend without leaving his home.

Tom Antion records his sold-out telephone seminars on an inexpensive tape recorder connected through a simple plug he bought at Radio Shack for less than $20. Then he dubs the tapes and sells them.

When we record our Internet radio show, we use a great little gizmo called a telephone logger patch, the Dynametric TLP 102. It gives you terrific telephone clarity and only costs about $50.

You certainly don't need to rent a studio or sell a book to a traditional publisher.

Do the folks in the media care that your book is self-published or that you produced your audio series on equipment you bought at a garage sale down the street?

Nope.

All they know is that you've done it. And that's what really matters.

See Appendix B for some resources that will help you become a publishing "do-it-yourselfer."

Having a professional looking product on your website, or including a list of e-books you've published (even self- published) with your media kit won't guarantee that you'll get the coverage (i.e. publicity) that you're looking for.

But it will certainly go a long way toward building your credibility with media decision-makers, and removing the natural skepticism that's part of every journalist's emotional make-up.

For more information, get Joan Stewart's excellent *Special Report #6: How to Write How-to Articles that Position You as an Expert.*

It tells you:

- 56 ideas for great headlines
- How to choose a topic
- How to use bullet points
- The key elements of an identifier paragraph
- The structure of a good article
- How to make and use reprints
- Where to find publications that want your articles

Click on www.get-free-publicity.com/publicityhound.html for ordering information.

Dan Janal also offers an invaluable service that puts experts and reporters together quickly. It's called PRLeads, and he described it for us recently on our radio show.

Everyday I get upwards of a hundred of requests from reporters who are writing articles and are desperate to find experts to give their stories credibility.

I find out the reporter's name, what paper they're writing for, and the deadline. I also get a short description of the article and the kind of information they are looking for. Then I send that information to my clients who match that profile: psychologists, doctors, authors, speakers and management consultants, for instance.

I have more than 400 clients now in less than two years, and as I said before, there are a lot of doctors, VPs and so on. But I also have people who have had significant life experiences.

I have one woman who's a 71-year-old retiree who has walked the Appalachian Trail and she does motivational speeches on how the elderly can still lead a very active life. She signed up for the service one day and she got into the New York Times the very next day.

It really is amazing how much information reporters need to build a story, and if you have the information they want, you're golden. It's a match made in heaven.

As we recorded our interview, it was one week after the Space Shuttle Columbia disaster. In situations like that, reporters need to find an expert fast. So PRLeads provides a valuable services to journalists.

On the Monday after the disaster for the shuttle, I got a number of leads from the top publications looking for experts in flights and avionics. Several computer magazines called looking for experts on data backups, wanting to know if the information from the shuttle could be transferred to a computer system on the ground. And I do have experts in that field, and the reporters ate it up. Some of my experts will wind up on the front page of these computer publications.

You can learn more about Dan Janal's PRLeads service by visiting www.prleads.com.

Be forewarned though—Dan is very meticulous about whom he chooses for his "expert's directory."

Raising Your Media Profile

Even if you don't have books or other products that you've created, you can still build a reputation as expert. Once you do, you'll find yourself getting on the air or in print… not just once, but over and over and over again…

Pat Rodgers shares this success story on how media attention, and the publicity it brings with it, can have such a huge impact on your bottom line.

> There was this handyman, a regular handyman, who owned a very, very small chain of independent lumberyards—two or three stores. It was back in the mid-70s when talk radio was kind of new, fresh, and green, and the radio station needed an expert handyman. The big guys didn't want to mess with it. 'We can't afford the time.' But suddenly this guy comes forward. He was a fairly consistent advertiser, but no big money.
>
> But he became known as <u>the</u> handyman, just by being on the air once a week. That's it. He was on an hour a week, then he was on the air for an hour and a half a week, and before you know it… and I do mean before you know it… it took a couple of years, I guess, he became known as THE handyman in the community.
>
> He had to confront a war of two home centers in this city… There was one other handyman on the air. He still only owned two or three little stores… A little lumber, a little hardware… And all of sudden millions of advertising dollars were being poured into this city by two behemoth chains battling it out for the homes market. But he just kept going on the air… the happy handyman.
>
> Well, when it finally came down to it and the dust settled,

*one of the big guys was out of business. I mean there were
a lot of empty buildings around the city with their name on
them. Guess who survived? The other chain of course, after
spending millions and millions of dollars. But so did this radio
handyman. I believe he did it because he established himself
as the expert of trust and he commercially backed it up with
intelligent marketing. In fact, he's in his eighties now, and
he's still doing it.*

It's all about being a resource for the person who is at the micro-
phone. The more obvious you make it that your goal is to help them,
to be a resource they can call on, the more often they'll use you.

Pat says you should also let them know that they can give you a call
anytime.

*If you can get on a talk show producer's Rolodex and if
you can win the trust of the talk show host... If they like
you—even if they don't agree with you, if they just like engaging you—if they like what happened when you were on
the air, you'll get a lot of airtime.*

*This used to happen all the time with people who were stock
market experts particularly. The stock market tends to be out
of the sphere of understanding of most talk show hosts.*

*Also, anything dealing with psychological problems when
there's a major story in the news where tragically people are
emotionally troubled and do bad things. To be able to find
an expert in that field... That kind of person ends up being in
the Rolodex, and the first thing we'll say when we see a story
is 'Call So-and-So. They'll have a take on that.' When you
start building that kind of credibility, you're in great shape.*

Frank Guerra and Joan Stewart have some more insights on this
highly effective strategy of positioning yourself as an expert, which
you may be surprised to learn isn't always as difficult as you might
think. Frank says

*One of the things to do is get into the so-called expert's
directory or the resource directory. Basically, it's a list or it
might be a small book of names that they keep in news-*

rooms, so that whenever something happens on a particular topic, they have a particular person to call on who can speak with intelligence on that topic.

Those things—credentials in a media kit or news release—should be designed in a certain way. Very simple. It should say 'We are experts in the following.' And list them... with maybe a one-line description of what those different categories are.

If you are an agency, university, or someone who represents a number of experts, such as authors, you can list the expert that you would make available and the phone number that they would call. The news folks are always pressed into trying to find the expert that can address a topic. If you make that easy for them, they will see you as a regular resource.

Joan Stewart notes that there's a good reason why you see so many college professors quoted on radio, TV or in print.

Universities have written the book on how to do expert directories. Most colleges and universities send them out regularly every year. It's nothing more than a directory of college professors and staff people and administrators who are experts in different areas.

As a reporter, I have a stack of those expert directories on my desk. When I was assigned a story that would just fall out of the sky and I had to have it done in an hour and a half and I didn't know where to go to, I'd pick up an experts directory and call one of the professors and quote them. That's why [professors] are quoted all the time.

Writing and Distributing Articles, Reports, and Papers

Publishing articles, particularly offline, can be a huge source of credibility—and new subscribers.

As we mentioned earlier, Dr. Kevin Nunley has built a large part of his business by producing articles and getting them into the hands of editors.

In fact, he says it was the only kind of promotion he did for the first three years his business existed.

> I tell people my business was built entirely with sending out free articles and that's exactly the way that it works.

> We do a lot of writing at www.drnunley.com. A lot of people come to us and we write articles for them and then send them out to email newsletters and websites. It's wonderful promotion.

Kevin and other people who deliver articles and press releases are beginning to use autoresponders in a way that hasn't been done before.

Once again, you're dealing with media people who are always pressed for time. You can send them a short press release, or an article synopsis, inquiring if they'd like more information. Supply them with an autoresponder that contains a copy of the article or media kit they need. All they have to do is click on a link, and then send a blank email.

> That's an excellent idea. And do you know what else we do a lot?

> We use articles to get people to sign up for free mini-courses, and that's how we get them to subscribe to a newsletter. I've had tremendous success with that.

> And in a sense, you can even make your articles do double-duty for you. You can bunch some of them together into one of the mini-courses I just mentioned.

> Of course each article has some of your promotional materials embedded in it, and that works really well.

> I've had some mini-courses out there for several years now, and I went to check the stats on it just the other day. Over 8,000 had subscribed to it and actually stayed on the list. This has been over the course of a couple of years so the thing has basically run on its own.

*A friend of mine has a business called www.sevenlessonscou
rses.com, and we have over a dozen courses there right now.
For a small fee you can offer one of those on your site to get
people to subscribe to your newsletter.*

*All you do is add some script to your web page and put your
five line ad in the box there where people sign up and away
you go. It's marvelous if you don't like to write or you don't
have time to write.*

Truth is, most people hate to write. So there are services like www.
elance.com where you can find those kinds of services, and they're
relatively inexpensive. Kevin adds,

All you have to do is jot something down in very rough form and
have a writer polish it up for you. Kevin says it's easy for a professional writer to take a page of notes on how to do something and
turn that into a nice polished article.

*We have some packages where we do the writing and the
promotion. We tie a whole bunch of different strategies
together into one affordable package and for a number of
years now those have been our really big sellers, so we do
and then we throw in free advice and counseling along the
way.*

"Special Reports"

As mentioned earlier, you should never do a broadcast media appearance without offering something you can give to listeners or
viewers—if they'll just ask you for it.

Tips lists and checklists are great. So are booklets and "special reports."

What are special reports?

Special reports are simply "how to" articles stretched into longer
form. Joan Stewart has raised this promotion vehicle to an art form,
and even turned it into a more-than-modest profit center. Her
Special Reports are five pages each, $9.00 per report, and she offers

forty-three of them on her website at www.get-free-publicity.com/publicityhound.html

You don't have to sell them though, like Joan does. You can give yours away as a "service" to people who want more information about the topic of your radio or TV appearance.

There are other ways to distribute them too.

Now, you may be thinking, "This sounds like too much of a writing job for me. It's got to be beyond my capability."

Enter the company we mentioned above: Elance.

If you're not already familiar with Elance, go to www.elance.com and check out their services.

"Elance" of course, is a combination of the words "electronic" and "freelance." Or possibly "e-commerce" and "freelance."

Regardless, they're the net's premier way to find people who will do what you can't or don't want to.

You can find someone there who will ghostwrite for you.

You put your project up for bid, and within hours qualified vendors post their prices. It's all done on the web, via email.

We used Elance to transcribe the interviews that are in this book.

Anyway, once you've either written your special report, or farmed it out to a ghostwriter, you can start distributing it.

- Offer it to audiences at your speaking engagements (get their email address and send it to them electronically, or direct them to a web page where they can get it—and sign up for your newsletter)
- Send them to clients as a thank you
- Send a shorter version of your special report to the media, and mention at the end of the article, in the identifier paragraph, that you have special reports on similar topics at your website.
- Offer excerpts or a shorter version of your report to publishers of print and online newsletters.
- As previously mentioned, offer them to audiences when you are interviewed in the electronic media.

For more information on creating special reports and promoting yourself through them, get Joan Stewart's (guess what) *Special Report #20: How to Write and Market Profitable Special Reports*, which explains:

- Why special reports are the easiest, most profitable product you can create
- Who can write them and what to do if you can't write
- Where to start and how to choose a format
- Writing tips
- Technical considerations
- How to price them and market them
  How to create a flier that advertises your special reports

Marcia Yudkin's e-book, *Profiting from Booklets and Special Reports*, is another excellent resource. Marcia explains which formats have the highest perceived value, precisely how to create an information item to be printed or downloaded and what to do to market it. www.get-free-publicity.com/yudkin.html

Part 2
Turning Low-Tech into High Traffic

Chapter 6

All Hail the "Snail"—
The Importance of "Going Postal"

Postcards

Alex Mandossian is one of the top marketing experts anywhere.

Mandossian has helped direct the marketing efforts of some of the world's best-known companies: Dale Carnegie, Anthony Robbins, Nightingale Conan Corporation, etc.

His most productive and profitable online product teaches people how to build their business by marketing with postcards.

But he's also proficient at using other "low-tech" vehicles to make online money. Turning "bricks" into clicks and clicks into cash, in other words.

In fact, he was the one who suggested using the word "bricks" to symbolize any offline strategy, tactic, or technique an entrepreneur might use to get more "clicks" on their website.

This is a man who knows as much as anybody—possibly *more* than anybody—about converting browsers to buyers.

And when we say browsers, we're not talking about Web browsers like Netscape, Internet Explorer, or Safari.

We're talking about people who may come to your website or walk into your business, and then start looking around.

How do you get those people to stop looking and start buying?

Keep reading and you'll find out.

To Get Clicks, Get "Naked"

No, we're not talking about porn here. Alex uses the word "naked" to describe postcard marketing, and he says it's a great way to "seduce" people to visit your website so you can sign them up as subscribers.

The postcard is naked mail. It's not clothed in an envelope. The beauty of it is that, unlike email, it's not virtual, so you see more than a subject line.

Since it's not clothed in an envelope, so you don't need teaser copy on the envelope.

There are some copywriters that you pay $25,000 per letter. They'll torture themselves just trying to figure out how to get the envelope open.

Well, with the postcard, you don't need that. It gets past the email box, because it sneaks in through the snail-mail box. It's physical, and there's no delete key that can delete it forever into cyberspace.

It can be a billboard by mail. You know those billboards you see on the side of the freeway? A postcard is a miniature billboard by mail.

It's also a website by mail, because it's pictorial. Letters cost a fortune, just the postage alone. But if you added color to a letter, it costs a fortune. When you get a Sharper Image catalog, it's very colorful, but it also cost a lot of money.

A postcard doesn't. You just decide. The hand lifts the postcard, you read the billboard, which is the picture side, you turn it over, which is the face side, and within ten seconds, you've decided whether you want to take action or not.

For instance, ah-ha.com sent out a postcard to a dear friend of mine, Brett Ridgeway, who runs TWIPress.com. They have a lot of rare books and tapes.

It was a 4-inch by 6-inch postcard. It said 'ah-ha.com—only the good stuff.'

So he shrugged his shoulders. He turned it over, and it said 'Dear Brett Ridgeway.' So it was personalized.

It continued, 'We miss you. The past few months have brought many changes. Our traffic has soared, and our account management system has been updated. We have detailed reporting for billing, key listings, banner campaigns, and more. Our help section has even expanded to include useful information and live...'

Live. They had live online assistance, which meant they had people sitting in chairs with headsets in a building somewhere. That made this a 'brick' campaign, right?

So the postcard continued, 'Reopen your account today, and receive, (a) no signup fee, (b) one month free logo links, and (c) free keyword creation. It's easy. Just email us at cs@ah-ha.com.'

And they even gave the phone number. And it also said 'Or you can even visit us at ah-ha.com.'

Ah-ha is a pure Internet marketer, but they're sending Brett a postcard. And what they're trying to do there is re-activate Brett, because they realize that Brett has probably put them on the spam filter. So every time he gets something from ah-ha, and sees it on the subject line, he probably deletes it, so they're sneaking in through the mailbox.

Alex also likes a postcard he recently saw from AllBooksForLess.com. On the billboard side, there's a picture of a giant alligator with its mouth open, it says, "Amazon. A nice place to visit, but you wouldn't want to buy there."

Then they try to 'seduce' you with an offer. It says, 'Now through December 15th, buy two books at AllBooksForLess.com, and your third book is free.'

So, basically, it's buy two, get one free.

On the backside is my address, and then it says,

'Sure, Amazon.com is an exotic place to look around, but those prices will eat you alive. That's why, before you buy, you should check out www.allbooksforless.com.'

And it gives you the URL and it tells you when the offer ends, and on this entire postcard, there's no phone number. It's amazing. The postcard is designed just to get you online.

You may be thinking to yourself right now, "What's the difference between that and spam?" Alex agrees,

It's kind of like spam, only there's no spam filter with the mailman. That's illegal. It's a felony. He can't throw it away. And that's why offline marketing, specifically the postcard, is very powerful, because you know your card will reach your recipient. You don't have that confidence with email.

You won't be surprised to learn that Alex uses postcards extensively to promote his own website and products. He says,

Now picture this. One of my customers has just spent $247.00 for the three-ring binder version of my 'Marketing With Postcards' course. The binders have a lot of thump value. It's a pound and a half worth of material. Or they spend $147.00 for the CD-ROM, and of course they save a hundred bucks because I don't have to print it up and they just get the disc.

Well, a week after that, they get this postcard. It's 4 inches by 6. There's a violinist, and it says, 'Beautiful music doesn't just happen.' And there's a handwritten note, by me.

This one says, 'June 6, 2003, Hi John. Now that you're learning how to profit with postcards, I want to show you how to become a world-class copywriter for less than 80 dollars. To get the full story, visit www.copywritingcoach.com. Best, Alex.'

Personal note from me. They just bought from me. So what's this? It's 23 cents postage; it's about 10 seconds of my time. I have a bunch of them pre-stamped, and would you believe, and would you believe—one out of twenty people who get

*this card pay me eighty dollars. One out of twenty. That post-
card cost me about 30 cents to mail. So 30 cents times 20 is
six dollars, and I get 80 dollars back.*

*So that's a 5% conversion rate, and I'm getting that conver-
sion because they're already my customers. And it's a handwritten postcard.*

*If you have more than one product, that second product can
be sent out either by direct mail or by postcard with a handwritten note, and you will be surprised at the results. Because
they just bought from you and they've never received postcards or any kind of direct mail from online marketers.*

But even a postcard from a huge corporation, like Citibank, can
make an impression when it arrives in the mailbox. Alex shares this
example.

*This is from Citibank. This is a 6-inch by 9-inch postcard. It's
pure red. This is the billboard side. This is a great headline. All
it says is 'Time isn't your enemy. Wasting time is.'*

*When you turn it over it says 'Make friends with your
time. Citibank Account Online. Save time with Account Online today. Have your Citicard handy, and go to
www.accountonline.com. Number one: Click on register
now. Number two: click on account information. Number
three: choose your user ID and password. It's quick and easy.
www.accountonline.com'*

*Look at the power of that. It's almost like sending an email,
but this is an email by mail, and it's almost like an HTML
email by mail, because it's in full color, and it's getting attention.*

*It's fabulous what they're doing, and there's no one reading
this book that is unable to do this. Anyone can do this for
as little out the door. The postage is 23 cents, you can get a
good postcard printer to print up postcards, four color, both
sides, for about eight cents. So you're looking at about 31
cents total, and it's nothing more than a little bit of account-*

ing. You can hire somebody for ten bucks an hour to do it, and watch the orders come in.

If you send 6x9's in bulk, they're under 23 cents. Bulk mail is very good if you have no hurry or rush, but you have to have a good address, because it won't come back to you if the address is no good. If it's your own customer, I always send bulk; in fact I send it the day I get the order, because I know it will get there in about a week and a half.

But if it's a mailing list I'm buying, I don't send bulk. I send first class so I can know which ones aren't getting delivered.

There are a number of places you can go, even some online, to have postcards printed. There's www.postcardkingdom.com, also www.postcardpower.com.

Some of the best-known Internet marketers have used Alex's offline techniques. Yanik Silver is among them. Yanik was one of the pioneers in marketing e-books, and his publications *Million Dollar Emails, Instant Sales Letters,* and *Autoresponder Magic* are considered classics.

But recently, when he wanted to promote www.webcopysecrets.com, he used postcards as one of his marketing strategies.

They send a six-inch by nine-inch postcard, and really it's a web page. It says, "Here's exactly how to write web copy that makes the sale." And then it gives about 500 words about how successful web marketers like Jonathan Mizel, Marlon Sanders, Joe Vitale, Jim Edwards, and Dean Jackson have built their businesses by writing great web copy.

When you turn it over, there are some testimonials.

But there's something else that makes this card different. In fact, according to Mandossian, it's ingenious.

This postcard was actually sent to me by one of their affiliates. So this card is promoting through an affiliate program, and it's very, very simple.

It says, 'Go to www.webcopysecrets.com/ewi. They've hard-

coded that URL, that extension, so once you go there, it's an affiliate link.

In this case it's my friend Brett Ridgeway again. He is going to get the commission after this postcard goes out. How smart is that?

Anyone who has an affiliate program can do this, and who has ever heard of getting postcards that are like web pages by mail? Very, very few of us do it

This is 'bricks and clicks' marketing, and I've got news for you. These are the early years for clicks and bricks marketing. Anyone who starts using some of these techniques <u>now</u> will be ahead of the curve and will make a lot more money at very, very little cost.

Most of us think about affiliate programs on the net. You make a commission when you sell someone else's e-book, or software, or seminar.

But big companies are also using affiliate programs creatively, and they're doing it through postcards. Here's another example from Alex Mandossian.

Now I'm sure if anyone is living, and can fog up a mirror, has probably gotten something from American Express. They are very good postcard marketers. They have been a client of mine for about a year and a half, and I do a little of their business and copy-writing design.

They have one postcard that promotes 'Offer Zone'. It's a big card, 6 inches by 9 inches, and it says, 'Free shipping and handling for the holidays. We're in the giving mood, too. AmericanExpress.com.'

When you turn it over, and it says, 'Get free shipping and handling on holiday gifts at Offer Zone,' and it talks about what's happening this holiday season.

This was sent to me sometime in November, so it was priming the pump for December, before Thanksgiving. And then the URL is www.AmericanExpress.com/offerzone.

And here's something that's extremely important. There is not one phone number anywhere on this card.

And here's something else that's critical.

Over to the right, it has all the affiliate partners, who probably helped pay for the mailing. It says 'Free shipping and handling for Bloomingdales.com, Clinique.com, DesignerRoulette.com, Drugstore.com, Origins.com, Tourneau.com.'

So what does that mean? These case studies are for big, big companies. How does this apply to us? Alex explains further.

Let's say you have thousands of affiliates, and you go to seven of them, and you say, 'Joe, I've got a deal for you.' Or I go to you and say, 'How would you like to market with postcards and generate 40% commission on every postcard course I sell? You're an affiliate. Here's what I'd like you to do.

I'm going to hard code my site, and it's going to say www.m arketingwithpostcards.com/joel, and that's going to be your affiliate link. So anyone who types in that URL will be redirected to Marketing With Postcards. A cookie goes on their computer, and Joe gets credit if there's a sale there.

However, what if I have thousands of affiliates, and I want to promote one particular person?

Well, the postcard can actually have five or six different websites. ALL of them share in the payment. All of them also share in the expense. All of a sudden, thirty or thirty-one cents becomes five cents.

There are hundreds more tactics offered in Alex Mandossian's course. You can learn more about it at www.marketingwithpostcards.com.

Why Snail Mail is So Powerful

All of us who market through permission based email know that we'll never get one hundred percent of our subscribers to even open our e-zine. Some will get ignored. Some get deleted by spam filters.

But with postcards and direct mail, there is no delete key. It takes effort to throw it away, and it does get looked at—even if only for a few seconds before it sails into the circular file. But you can bet that most people at least glance at it. Most will look at the picture and probably even read the message. That's the sheer power of it. And when you get more readers, you're bound to get more results.

The Business Reply Card

You know when you buy an electronic item of any kind, let's say a Palm Pilot or a digital camera or a computer, they have these little business reply cards inside the box? They have a bunch of questions, and they say it's your warranty card, but really, they just want to get demographic or geographic information from you?

Those are called business reply cards. They can be a little annoying, but a lot of people fill them out and send them in.

Well, guess what. Those business reply cards, or BRCs can be powerful tools (or "bricks") for building your list. Alex Mandossian remembers one that he got recently.

I bought something from US Robotics… 3-Com… and in the box was a post-purchase survey.

Here's the beauty of this survey: no human interaction. No human touch.

I can't imagine the amount of money and time they save because of this. And I'll tell everyone how it can apply to them, too.

On one part of the card you have the business reply information, no postage necessary, which you'll dump in the mailbox.

Then you open that fold, and on the other part of the card you have all the questions. You know, thank you for your purchase, please give the model number, etc.

Well, on the fourth panel, it says, 'Your feedback is important to us.' Now that is a bad headline. Let me tell you something that out-pulls that. 'We need your advice.' People don't like to give feedback as much as they like to give unsolicited advice. Any married couple knows that.

So at this point, if I were to change this card, I would say, 'We need your advice,' or 'Your advice means much to us.' In any case, it says, 'We want to make our products even better. Please answer the questions on the reverse side of this card, fold it in half, seal it, tape it, and then mail it in. Or, register online at www.3-com.com/homeconnect/register.

So what happens? A lot of people won't want to drop it in the mail, because they don't want to go to a post office. But they're sitting right there at their home computer, so they say, 'Okay, I'm going to do my warranty thing online.'

How does this apply? Very simple.

What you do is have a little questionnaire, and you have them fill out their address. Now, they already did that with their credit card purchase, but you have them fill it out again.

When they give you that and send it in, you send them a postcard, thank them for what they did, giving you feedback, and give them a surprise gift.

I recommend brick and mortar, a special report, something physical.

Now think about this.

What's more of a headache to read? A 200-page PDF that you have to read as you sit at your computer or download and print? Or something physical, in hard copy, where all you have to do is flip pages and start highlighting?

Well, of course the PDF takes more effort, because you have to print it, or you have to go to Kinko's. A lot of people feel that's a burden.

But when I get something physical, it's a joy. It's like getting a book.

So I do surveys with some of my products, and I have many of my clients do the same thing, and send them a surprise bonus gift.

And that surprise bonus gift can — in and of itself — have one of these BRC cards, which are dirt-cheap, and the postage costs less than a postcard: 20 cents for the reply.

Or, you can do an online poll, and then physically send them a book. Either way, it's clicks and bricks. Either they're dong a poll online, and you're sending them a physical gift, or you're sending them a postcard, and you're sending them a virtual gift or a physical gift. I always like the physical gift, especially if they've paid me money, because it makes the relationship more real.

So, it's using offline techniques to build relationships. It's almost like dating. The goal is to get to that second or third date, so you can date exclusively, get married, and hopefully have children.

In the bricks and clicks method, with 3Com using a BRC, or business reply card, is just brilliant

Or better yet, do some kind of an up-sell, where they pick up an item online and you give them a special password-pro-tected site as a bonus. You will get the click from that order. Because they're going to open that. They just paid good money to buy something from you. When they open it gives them another reason to come back to you as a surprise gift, and they will.

I've had as high as 55% of the people click to get the special bonus gift for free. Because number one, it's a surprise. And number two, because it is free.

But make it important. Don't make it something that is of zero value. Make it very, very important.

Catalog Booklets: Thousands of Clicks with One Mailing

Here's another tactic Alex Mandossian suggests. It's called the Catalog Booklet.

Suppose you sell a bunch of products. This is how to get thousands of clicks with one mailing. It's like a co-op.

Any Internet marketer who has more than twenty friends online right now and has products to sell could do this immediately.

Alex says American Express is currently using this tactic, and doing it very well.

> It's a book. It's not a postcard, like those postcard packets. It's an actual book, and when I'm looking at the book it says
>
> 'Point. Click. Save.'
>
> And the URL is www.americanexpress.com/offerzone.
>
> This is the booklet, and when I open the booklet I see offers from Time-Life.
>
> 'Save 20% on your first purchase of $75.00 or more.'
>
> I see an offer from Viking Press.
>
> 'Free deluxe travel bag with purchase of Viking travel products.'
>
> Now, what's different about this?
>
> There's not one phone number on it. Not one. You go to www.vikingoffice.com and the promo code—that's key—the promo code is AMEX. That's the affiliate code.
>
> Same thing for Time-Life. You go to www.timelife.com/amex and the promo code is AMEXDS. That's how you're getting the discount.
>
> Anybody who knows 20 marketers can put this together and get their offer in the book for free. Because I'm sure you can get 19 people to pay for the cost of the book and the mailing.

This thing is physical. Just make it a very compelling offer and again.

You can easily send a perfectly bound book like this to a host of customers. In fact, the best place to send it is to everybody's database.

Let's say you have 20 marketers who are participating. We're going to purge and make sure we're not sending to the same person. It's a co-op mailing. That's like co-registration, only it's by mail.

So that's a brick and mortar concept. American Express is a very savvy 'clicks and bricks marketer,' and they're using all their vendors, putting it in a book, and sending it out at Christmastime.

What do I look for during Christmastime? I look for savings. And I love the cover of the book. Point. Click. Save.

And listen to this: many offers, one address. They're building a brand, www.americanexpress.com/offerzone. Awesome, awesome technique.

Direct Mail

Unlike a postcard, direct mail requires an envelope and sometimes something of value or something personal. Like a postcard, however, direct mail lets you sneak in more clicks via the mailbox.

Alex Mandossian once again supplies this example.

This is written by one of my colleagues, Trevor Levine. He's done a lot of copywriting for Cory Rudl, who's one of the richer online marketers at www.marketingtips.com.

The goal with this particular direct mail piece is to get a referral. Let's say you're a copywriter, or a website designer, or an HTML programmer, or a database builder, or you have a professional service. This is March 11, 2002. It says:

'Dear Alex. Why are you receiving this check?'

And I'm thinking to myself, 'What check?'

And I look and it says Heritage House, that's my company. $150.00. And it's signed by Trevor Levine. It says, 'Why are you receiving this check?' And the check is stapled to the cover letter.

It continues.

'It's just to show you how easy it is to collect referral fees from us, with virtually no work on your part. Why $150.00? Because that's the referral fee you'll earn on a thousand dollar copywriting job.' Obviously he's paying 15%, right? 'In fact, for each referral you send you'll receive 15% of the gross for the first 6 months your referral works with us. Since I know I trust you, I'm sending you this check on the honor system.

Please don't cash it yet. Instead keep it on your desk in good faith, in advance and use it for the next job you send us.'

So in other words, just like a bartender does, he's salting the tipping jar. He's giving me $150 to motivate me to send him referrals. He's an offline copywriter. He does virtual copy. And he has www.marketingexperts.com. But he's sending me a letter with a check. Believe me, do you think I'll send business to him? How motivating is that?

He did that to a bunch of folks. And they had the same reaction. It's a brilliant, brilliant example.

It's almost like a tip, but the tip comes before the service.

For instance, when I go to a hotel I always tip the concierge first. People say, 'Why do you do that?' Well, when you tip afterwards, it's almost like you're tipping for services rendered, but the best way to get better services, whether it's a referral or any type of service, I like to pre-tip. And it works like a charm. If anything, there's pressure or guilt, and they remember your name.

So that's what Trevor is really doing. He's tipping in advance to get a commission. On the honor system. I'm not going to cash that check. I know him; he's a friend of mine. So you don't do that with strangers, but what a great way to get referrals from people who know, like and trust you.

Here's another tactic Alex shared. This is from wine.com.

Now wine.com is a pure online player. They sell wine online. You save money buy purchasing through them.

They send a letter. It's a cover letter. It's hand signed by their regional sales manager. And it says, 'Don't wait until the last minute to get your corporate holiday gift giving done. Let us help you become a hero this holiday.' It has a few testimonials, talks about the mission of wine.com.

But most important, if you use the code on the letter you get a 10% discount. The code is CORPHOLIDAY.

So you see there's always some type of offer and then they're giving you something of value.

But to get it, you have to take the letter, go to your desk, and type it into the browser.

In other words, they've just used a 'brick' to get you to click.

"It's the future of the Internet," Mandossian says.

Start thinking offline. Start thinking bricks.

Bricks to clicks.

Clicks to cash.

Bonus Gifts

This is a tactic that may be totally unique to Alex Mandossian. He calls it "the bonus gift cover letter."

And he uses it to cross sell without package inserts.

When you get a product, typically you'll get all the bonus gifts in the product. You'll get maybe a "drop card" package insert in the product as well.

But there's no "isolation factor."

Mandossian claims the isolation factor is critical to success.

Do you know why infomercials work? Because there are no prime time shows next to them. It's irritating when you want to watch a show and you get a commercial. But at 2 o'clock in the morning when your resistance is low, these infomercials are isolated. And a guy by the name of Alvin Eicoff proved it.

Non-primetime slots are the best TV and radio times for direct response advertising. Not primetime. And best of all, they're cheaper.

The isolation factor also works with bonus gifts and with offers.

So, I mentioned the package insert. This is a brick and mortar tactic.

What I do is I give $650 in bonus gifts. I have them fax back the bonus gift reply form that's in my course. It's on the inside cover of my course. I tell them to take it out, fax it back to me. I'm not giving it away as garbage.

They have to do something and work for that bonus. I make them do that for two reasons.

To read the course, or at least to open the box so it doesn't collect dust—because it does have a lifetime guarantee.

And number 2, so I can certify and hand sign the gifts.

I give them an envelope that looks like a FedEx envelope. There's a cover letter in there along with their certificates and bonus gifts. I give numerous bonus gifts, but the P.S is what's really interesting about it.

Aside from giving the bonus gifts separately, in my P.S. I write:

'If you want to increase the pulling power of all your marketing communications and become a world-class copywriter for less than $80, take a moment to visit www.copywritingcoach.com.'

Now, every single person who's looking at that insert just purchased 'Marketing with Postcards.' And what does post-card marketing involve? Copywriting! And I have a copywriting package at www.copywritingcoach.com and I'm urging them to check it out.

Number one, they like it because now they have a chance to learn something valuable from without paying a consulting fee. I don't come cheap at $350 an hour.

But I'm putting it in a very isolationist place—as a P.S. with the bonus gifts.

This not only gives them satisfaction. It gives them delight. We're delighting the customer. It's satisfaction when you put the bonus gifts with the package and they're opening the box and there are all the packages there.

They fax it to me, then I mail out the bonus gifts. It costs me an extra 65 cents, but the cover letter is my driver for the up-sell. I'm delighting them because their bonuses are separate, and I'm not overwhelming them.

And my offer in the P.S. is isolated and I'm telling them, 'Hey, you want to be a copywriter for less than 80 bucks, go to copywritingcoach.com.' No one that I know of so far has ever used that tactic. Everyone information publisher I know can use that tactic.

Chapter 7

"Phone-etics"—That Ringing Sound You Hear is the Cash Register

Teleseminars

We know a professional speaker who says, "I speak because I love it. I travel because I have to."

Even before American travelers went on "terrorist alert," there was a lot NOT to like about getting from business meeting to business meeting, conference to conference, convention to convention, seminar to seminar, speaking engagement to speaking engagement.

That's why distance learning has become a booming business.

Why hassle with plane connections, taxis and limos, sleeping in unfamiliar surroundings, and irregular meals when you can use technology to do what you need to do (and learn what you need to learn) without ever leaving the comfort of your home or office?

For a lot of people, video-conferencing is still on the other side of the horizon, but it will be here, for mass consumption, soon. Some companies, like 8point Communications, www.get-free-publicity.com/viewmail.html are already offering video services to the general public. We'll just mention it briefly here because most people haven't tried it yet.

But everybody has a telephone, and they know how to use it.

Enter the "teleseminar."

Dan Janal, who also operates www.prleads.com and

www.greatteleseminars.com, has become the acknowledged authori-
ty on teleseminars. During an interview for our radio show, we asked
him if they were becoming more and more prevalent.

*Well, it's a relatively new area. It's been used a lot by speak-
ers and coaches but not by a lot of businesses.*

*In fact, when we say the word 'teleseminars,' a lot of people
think it's a seminar delivered on television. That's not it, of
course. It's actually a done by telephone. So everyone has
access to that type of technology because everyone has this
phone or cell phone and they know how to use it. All they
have to do is call into a central conference line number and
punch in a pre-arranged code. The seminar leader delivers
the content.*

*So it can be twenty people or it can be two hundred people.
It could even be two thousand people all over the United
States all calling at their own convenience. Teleseminars are
really popular in the speaker community.*

*It seems funny now, but I used to be afraid of them because
they were different. It was just fear of the unknown.*

*But then I signed up for a couple, and I said, 'Hey this is actu-
ally pretty simple.' It's just like going to a real seminar, except
you can do it from the comfort and convenience from your
office or your home. Dial in a phone number and just listen.*

*Plus most teleseminars are interactive — so the clients get di-
rect access to an expert, and they can ask questions and get
answers in real time.*

*Teleseminars won't replace traditional seminars, but tradi-
tional seminars are expensive to produce, they're expensive
to get to, and a lot of companies these days won't spend the
money.*

*Suppose you want to do a sales training session inside your
organization? You might have people all over the country or
the state. Now they can just dial into the phone number and
get the training and motivation that they need in one simple*

setting, as opposed to driving or flying and taking half a day to get there.

Some people confuse teleseminars with conference calls, but Dan is quick to point out that there's a major difference.

For instance, if you call your local phone company and tell them you want to have a call with fifty people all listening in, they'll say, 'Oh, you need a conference call. That will cost you twelve cents a minute for every person on the line...'

That's one of the biggest rip offs that you can ever possibly imagine. You know, if you go to my website. www.greatteles eminars.com you can actually get a list of free phone conference centers, where you can have anywhere from 12 to 24 people coming in at anytime you want for no cost whatsoever. When I first heard about these things, I said 'There's got to be a catch—there's always a catch somewhere.' There's no catch. These conference center websites are basically paid by the telephone companies to just create traffic and usage on the telephone network. So they don't care if you're calling in on Sprint or MCI or Qwest or whatever, they just know that the rising tide will float all boats and if you have 50 people coming in and out of our bridge line for an hour there's a lot of money being generated for the phone companies and they get a cut of that. So you can actually produce a teleseminar for free.

When I first started there was no free teleconference line so I bought a telephone line rental for $250 a month. Now as a said before, you can probably find them for $10 a month or even free and they have many of the same features that I'm paying a lot of money for—my service still has a few features that still aren't available on the free services yet, so I'll stick with them. But for anyone starting out you can use a free service.

How much money can you make doing teleseminars? Dan was candid about the numbers.

A lot of speakers I know charge $25 or $35 dollars. If your *audience is the home based entrepreneur and the money is coming out of their own pockets, they won't pay much more than that. But if you're dealing with corporations, you can charge $79, $99, and $200.*

I have a client who's a sales trainer, he specializes in the car industry and he started doing his own teleseminars through me—through my Great Teleseminars company. In fact, he inspired me to start this company and offer this kind of service to speakers, experts, authors and companies that need to produce teleseminars but don't have the training or the staff or the know how, or just find it more convenient to outsource it to someone who knows what their doing.

So we were talking about pricing and stuff like that and I told him that most people are charging $20, $25 or $30 per seminar. He said, 'You know, my clients won't respect me if I charge that little. They'll think that it's a generic sales session. I'm dealing with highly trained, highly motivated professionals, so we have to charge all higher prices cause they'll perceive it as something more important.

So a couple of weeks later he came to me and said, you know were ready to do the seminar. I asked how many people had signed up? He said 20.

I thought, 'Poor guy, only 20 people. I'm not sure he would cover his costs. So I said 'How much are you charging them?'

He said $300. So he made $6000 for delivering his teleseminar. These were actually 2-one hour teleseminars. One on sales and one of leadership and management—and this was the material that he previously created. So it was great. He didn't have to spend any time creating new material, he just found a new audience and a new format and able to deliver that material and they found real value in it and he found a real gold mind—enough to make him $6,000 a month for 2 hours of work.

The upfront cash is just part of the potential revenue stream from teleseminars. If you record the session, you can turn it into an audio-cassette or CD and sell it.

This way the organization can buy the CD or the product for you or you can buy it yourself if you are an individual and listen to it when you are jogging or driving to work in the car. It's the ultimate in convenience.

Teleseminars usually average twenty to thirty people at around $20 to $25 per person, but as we saw in the example above, it depends on the presenter and the topic. Dan says he's had some teleseminars involving only three callers.

> It's a little bit embarrassing but hey, it was the wrong topic at the wrong time. I've done other teleseminars when I had 60 or 70 people come in. I think my most popular one featured Susan Harrow, who had written a book teaching people how to get on the Oprah Winfrey Show. Everyone wanted to do that, so I had more than sixty people paying to attend the event. Then a good number more ordered the CD or the cassette afterwards. So if you have a good topic the sky's the limit.

Generally, the one person organizes the teleseminar, collects the credit card information and gets the word out. That same person is often the one who interviews an expert guest.

> We call that the talk radio format. It's lively, and it's fun. You don't get tired of hearing one voice drowning on and on and on. We've all been in seminars where the teacher just talks for 45 minutes and you fall asleep. With teleseminars, you get plenty of give and take and it's a lot more interesting for everyone.

For more information on teleseminars, visit Dan's website, www.greatteleseminars.com

Teleseminars are cheap and easy, but you still have to promote them, get as many people as you can on the call, and then convert them to subscribers. We'll discuss promotion first.

Free or Paid?

You have the option of charging for your teleseminar, or letting people listen in for free.

Your decision, of course, depends on what you're trying to accomplish.

If your main goal is to build your list by attracting new people who don't know you, you're probably better off with free-or-low-cost events.

However, if you want to high quality people who are ready, even hungry to buy your products, then a paid teleseminar is much better.

Populating Your Teleseminar with Potential Subscribers

Alex Mandossian says he's using this low tech "brick" in a number of creative ways to generate more and more clicks—which he eventually turns into cash.

"I can't tell you," he says, "how well teleseminars and even webinars, which I do, build my business, send me online traffic, and really have created a lifestyle for me and my family that I am very grateful for."

Alex notes, however, that most people who do teleseminars don't get maximum productivity out of them.

That's because when they promote their teleseminar, all they do is have people reserve their spot through an autoresponder, and then give them a code they can use to log onto the call.

On the day of the teleseminar, they call in and listen. When the call is over, they hang up... possibly, never to be heard from again.

But there are plenty of opportunities before, during and after the event to recruit subscribers and turn them into lifelong customers.

Converting Listeners to Subscribers

We should stress, right up front, that you can't just add someone to your subscriber list just because they signed up for a teleseminar. That would be spamming.

But you can use some legitimate pre- and post-seminar techniques and incentives to get them to become subscribers.

Confirmation letter

When they register for the teleseminar, send a confirmation letter via autoresponder. Be sure to set up an autoresponder that will keep each name on a separate list for that particular event. We'll explain why that's important in a moment.

You can also mention explain in the confirmation letter that you often do other teleseminars on similar topics. They can be notified of such events by signing up for your newsletter.

Finally, your confirmation letter should include a signature file at the bottom that describes your newsletter and invites them to subscribe.

Website pop-ups

The confirmation letter should also direct them to a website which offers an outline of material to be covered in the teleseminar — a syllabus, if you will.

But there's also a pop-up box on the website which features an opportunity to subscribe.

When they're through looking at the website and they close it, they see another pop-up box. This one offers a free report.

There are more offers to subscribe embedded subtly in the free report, of course.

The main event

During the teleseminar itself be sure to mention your newsletter and your website. You can also talk about free reports, free e-books or other helpful information you have available to subscribers.

Alex Mandossian often talks about case studies and success stories in his teleseminars. Toward the end of the call, he always says something like:

*If you liked what you heard today, if you would like the actu-
al curriculum I've read from, if you would like the case studies
for all the things I talk about in the teleseminar; here's what
you do.*

*You go to a special website, where you will see something I
created just for this event. I encourage everyone to go there
and get all the information, case studies, everything I discuss
including the curriculum.*

*Anyone who wants all that just fills in their first name and
their email address, and they get the information via autoresponder.*

Here's a screenshot of the webpage Alex set up for a recent teleseminar.

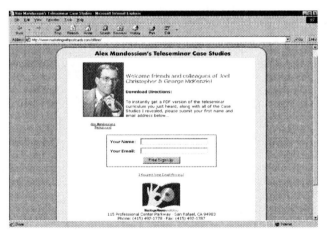

Naturally, after he captures the email addresses of those who sign up
at this page, he follows up using some of the techniques and incentives we've described above.

Here are some other ideas you can use once the teleseminar has
ended.

Streaming Audio Replays
Give anyone who listened to your teleseminar an opportunity to hear
it again.

Record the teleseminar, and then convert it to streaming audio. Send a follow up email to each person notifying them of a web page or website they can visit to listen. It's important to put the streaming audio link *on a webpage or website*. Here's why.

First, when they come to the website or page, they see a pop-up box inviting them to subscribe.

You also put sales material on the page itself, so they'll be seeing it, consciously or sub-consciously, while they listen to the streaming audio.

Of course, there's an exit pop-up, featuring an offer of your choice, when they're finished listening and they close the site.

Free teleseminar membership site

Someone who's interested in one teleseminar you've done may be interested in others. You can offer them a chance to hear previously recorded events through a free membership site.

Of course, to be eligible for the membership site, which features a library of recorded teleseminars, they have to subscribe to your list. Once they subscribe, they get a password that unlocks the library door, so to speak.

Subscriber-Only Free Teleseminars

You can also offer no-cost teleseminars. But they have to subscribe to your newsletter: that's the price of admission.

Other ways to build your list through teleseminars include:

Round-Robin Joint Ventures

Select a number of experts in a certain field — each with an opt-in list. Have the panelists all send emails to their subscribers inviting them to listen to the call.

During the call, each panelist can mention their website and newsletter and invite anyone who's not a subscriber to become one. You might call this technique, "list cross-pollenization."

Our friend Jason Potash of www.picktheirbrains.com and www.e-zineannouncer.com turbo-charged the cross-pollenization idea by inviting ten experts to come together on one call. Jason charged $37.00 for the teleseminar, and then shared the profits with the experts through an affiliate program. So every time one of the experts signed someone up for the teleseminar, they got a commission.

That, of course, motivated each expert on the panel to promote the teleseminar enthusiastically. One of them signed up more than four hundred people from his list. He made about $6000 in commissions in one night.

He probably also added some new subscribers to his list—as did many of the other panelists—through the cross-pollenization strategy. You can bet many of those subscribers later became customers, generating even more profits on the backend.

"Bring a friend" incentives
Offer a free product or some kind of gift to anyone who recruits a certain number of people who sign for the teleseminar. Anyone who signs up or refers that number or more receives a prize.

Contests
The person who signs up or refers the most teleseminars attendees gets a prize. Maybe also have second and third place winners.

Offer free coaching
Instead of offering products as prizes, offer your time. This can have an extremely high perceived value if you charge high consulting fees. You can also use free coaching as a "door prize" at live events like seminars. It not only serves to connect you to potential new subscribers/customers, but it's great free publicity to have your name mentioned in front of all the attendees.

Remember, the teleseminar is one of the most productive offline "bricks" anyone can use to generate more clicks—and more cash.

The Customer Callback

This is an extremely powerful telephone tactic takes only a few minutes—but it has a huge impact on present and future profits. It's one of Alex Mandossian's favorites.

Every time someone purchases something from me over $150.00, any time, I call him or her the same day. If I'm online for some reason on a Sunday, checking email, I'll call them on a Sunday. And you know what I tell them? First of all it floors them that I'm calling them.

I tell them, because I have some other brick and mortar stuff to follow, like the bonus gift reply form. I tell them, I'm calling you just to confirm that it was you indeed who purchased the course.

And then they feel, wow, yeah it was me. There's no fraud involved.

I say, 'Great, this is Alex Mandossian, and I'm the author of the book and I'm just calling to let you know, when you get the course, open the UPS box—see, I'm giving him imagery via my voice—open the box, and don't let it collect dust because it is guaranteed for life and I don't want it returned.

I want you to read it. Look on the inside cover and you'll see an 8-1/2 by 11 sheet of paper that's called the Bonus Gift Reply form. Fax it back to me and you'll get $650 worth of bonus gifts, certified and signed by me, from my office in San Francisco.

And the third reason I'm calling is to demonstrate that this is the beginning of our relationship, not the end. If you have any questions I'm definitely accessible to you by email at alex @marketingwithpostcards.com, or phone at 415-492-1778.

Now, people cringe, they wonder how you can give them your phone number. Do you know how many people call me? Practically none. But the fact that I did that means everything.

Gary Halbert used to talk about that, and I think he still does it. For testimonials put the phone number because it makes it look more credible. I used to do that with my direct mail letters, and with business-to-business mail it's great, because I don't care if they call me at the office. Maybe it's a new customer we can network with. Well, people never called. Just because the phone number is there doesn't mean they're going to call. But it gives them this sense of assurance.

Like, if you're getting an IPO offering of some kind, if that thing is only one page, you're going to have second thoughts about it. But if that thing is like 300 pages, you're not going to read all of it, but you say, hey these guys have done their homework, even though you read only five or six pages. The same with the phone call.

I can't stress enough how this single technique has increased my lifetime value of customers, and I only tested it for about 9-10 months, but it took my average customer from $250.00 to over $750.00 in 90 days after the call. Why? They would join teleseminars. They would do coaching with me. They would call me for consulting, copywriting online and offline.

The call makes you special, so call your customers.

Now, some people say, I sell a hundred products a day. I can't call everybody. Great, give free teleseminars. Show them that you appreciate them because they're your customers; they're your inner circle. That's what Jonathan Mizel and I did with marketingbraindump.com. All the people on the call had purchased something from us or were on our opt-in list, and we said, now that you've given something to us and put filet mignon on our table, we're going to give back. We're going to share the wealth we've accumulated and hopefully you can benefit from it.

That definitely clicks and bricks, right?

The phone is a much more personal medium than email. You can have a relationship on the phone. It's very difficult to have one in email.

The Automated Callback

You don't even have to TALK to someone personally on the phone to impress him or her.

Sometimes all you have to do is leave a message on their voicemail.

Take this example, once again shared with us by Alex Mandossian.

Anyone who's in the direct selling business, MLM business, or network marketing, referral marketing, whatever you like to call it, is probably familiar with Cutting Edge magazine. And there are many ads placed in Cutting Edge magazine by network marketers.

Here's what they do. Before the ad deadline happens, you get an automated message that comes to you. But if you answer the phone, it doesn't leave the message. It ONLY triggers if the call goes to the answering machine.

And that's very, very important, because it's not considered a cold call. It's just a message.

A company called realcallworks has the technology. www.realcallworks.com. It's brilliant! Patented technology, and all the scripts are supposed to be less than 30 seconds to make them nice and brief and natural sounding.

So let's say that you were going to advertise in Cutting Edge magazine and I had your phone number. You get a call and it's an automated calling network that goes to the answering machine and it's in my voice, and it says, 'Hello, this is Bill from Cutting Edge media just calling to let you know that Friday the 11th is the last day to get your ad in for the final issue of Cutting Edge magazine. So give us a call and we'll get that space reserved for you. If you've never advertised before, or maybe you've advertised and it just didn't work, we will help you put together an ad that will work. So please call us. The number is 800-961-9297. That's 800-961-9297. Just ask for someone in Marketing Support.'

What a great way, and a special way, to get people saying, 'Wow, that was a little different spin.' And it costs you 25 cents. It's nothing. There are some startup fees and such, but I'm going to give a phone number. I am not an affiliate of this company. In fact, I cannot be when I'm giving this referral. I want to make that very clear. So, you ask for Mike Eliis at 800-353-1420, extension 171. You can just go to realcallworks.com, just like it sounds.

Bob Schwartz, a customer of mine, and a good friend, was

formerly with Cutting Edge media. He used Real Call to invite customers and prospects to their phone conferences. And listen to what Bob had to say. He says, 'Within 24 hours of the start of our Real Call campaign, at 9:30 am, we could quite literally generate $5,000.00 to $10,000.00 in sales.' Just like that. Obviously they're calling a few thousand people, but you can do it in a much smaller amount.

Remember, you're not talking to a live person. In fact, you're not talking at all. You record it, then it senses if there's a voicemail there, and it leaves a message. Why a message? Because that's not a nuisance.

Think about this too. When you're listening to a message, when you're checking your voicemail, you are generally more attentive than you are if you get a call in the middle of dinner, or if you get a call while doing other things. If you answer the phone yourself, and you hear that automated voice, you'll probably just screen it out or you might even hang up. But if you're listening to your messages, you're in a whole different frame of mind than when you've just been interrupted while you're focused on doing something else.

When're you're calling someone with a reminder, it's not annoying. In fact, most people will be pleased to hear from you. They'll think, 'Oh yeah, there's that teleseminar I paid for.'

It works especially well with existing customers who have already paid you. It's a very, very good investment.

Just the Fax

One of the joys of Internet marketing is the "automatic-systematic" factor.

Thanks to websites and autoresponders, you can market on the web while you sleep, and pitch prospects with sales letters while you've got your backside planted in the white sand beaches of Cancun. When those prospects buy, you don't even have to ship the product—they download it electronically and the money shows up in your bank account shortly thereafter.

Automatically, systematically.

Best of all, inexpensively.

What a wonderful way to do business.

Offline promotion, of course, requires more attention, maintenance, and cost. But there are still some technological marvels in the offline world that come close to the "automatic-systematic" methods of the Internet.

Welcome to broadcast fax marketing.

Think about it.

Internet marketing whiz kid Yanik Silver used this "low-tech tool" (our description, not his) to get a return on investment, or ROI, of 15-1.

In his manual, *How To Make Instant Sales and Immediate Profits Using Cheap Fax Advertising*, he explains how he once spent $418 dollars to fax a sales letter that reaped $35,717.00 in sales almost overnight.

Think about it. The average fax costs about one half the cost of a postcard, about one third the price of a stamp.

There are other advantages too.

Faxes are fast, easy to send from your computer, and they get noticed. They're also great for test marketing.

And like email, the results are almost immediate. With a well-done sales letter, you can start getting orders within minutes.

Plus, there are no printing costs like you'd have with a brochure or an advertising flyer.

How to Use Broadcast Faxes as Traffic- and List-building Tools

The same principle that works best online works best offline with fax marketing.

Offer them something for nothing. A giveaway.

Free report, free audio or video, free sample of a product.

Free subscription to your e-zine?

Why not? That's how you do it online, don't you? Except online you usually use a popup box.

A fax is the telephone equivalent of a popup box offering a free report when the visitor signs up for your e-zine. In this case, the fax directs them to a special web page where they can subscribe to your newsletter—and after that, an autoresponder sends them their free report, or provides instructions for collecting their audio, video or free product sample.

You can even set up a toll-free telephone number, with a recorded message, if that's appropriate.

The fax is another of Alex Mandossian's favorite "bricks."

> A fax is less expensive than a post card. You can get fax broadcasting for 5-6 cents. I've heard as low as 3 cents. A postcard, just postage alone, is 23 cents.
>
> So a fax broadcast is pretty darned powerful and it is going to the fax machine, which means they're going to see it before they see the mail. Very, very powerful.
>
> It's got to be used properly, though. Now the fax broadcast is an exceptional medium, not to sell products, but to do an auto-reminder. And it costs less than to mail a postcard.
>
> I'll give you an example. I got a call from a company that calls itself 'The Internet Support Group'. Now, I don't know what the Internet Support Group is. But I do know I have a domain name called cashtrap.net, which I didn't want to renew. It was coming up for renewal.
>
> I got a fax from this company. It specified the domain name, then listed their toll free number, their URL, and spelled out a deadline. And it also had a tracking number.
>
> The fax says, and I'm paraphrasing:
>
> 'In accordance with U.S. legal code, be advised that protecting a domain name or trademark owner from confusing or

conflicting domain name registrants is not the responsibility of the domain name registrar, and blah, blah, blah...'

It looks official. And then it says, in so many words,

'Look, you'd be crazy to give this thing up. It's yours right now. Call 1-800-919-3134.'

I got 3 of these official looking faxes from this company. I called. And I called to tell them, you guys are doing a great job.

Okay, so you're asking, 'What do domain names have to do with the brick world?' Nothing, really! But what I'm saying is, look how this company used fax broadcasting instead of sending an email.

I recently had a client with whom I did a face-to-face con-sultation, and he hired me for a day. I got an auto-reminder via fax from his assistant saying, 'We look forward to seeing you tomorrow at 8 am.' I loved it. That was a 'brick' auto-re-minder.

Back to the Internet Support Group. When domain names are expiring, these people are sending faxes out. It's a heck of a lot more powerful than spamming or emailing because it doesn't look like spam. But basically, it is spam. Who are these guys? I never heard of them.

Bottom line is, a fax is not spam. You can complain about it. You can get off the list. But it's not spam in the same sense that people on the Internet think of spam. It's not held in the same regard that spam is which is horrible, terrible.

Faxes aren't that way. In the case of the Internet Support Group, it just seemed as if they were letting me know as a courtesy reminder that my domain name was about to come up for renewal.

You see more than just the subject line. It takes work; you need to click something to see the email. And then you have to look at a frequency that's vibrating on the screen, which is very difficult on the eyes. And some people use fonts that are just illegible. You can't read them; it's very irritating. And many people don't have netiquette. So because of those things, email becomes a nuisance. With a fax, you just take it out of your fax machine, and you read it or it goes straight in the wastebasket. But you look at it. This one got my attention and it was good enough to make the case study with.

Alex and Jonathan Mizel recently teamed up on a joint venture that took advantage of the power of fax broadcasting.

They created a product called The Marketing Brain Dump.

They did a survey asking only one thing: "What's the single most important question you have about Internet marketing for the year 2002?"

They got back one-hundred-and-eighty replies. Many of them overlapped, so they cut the list down to fifty-two relevant, specific topics.

Then they "brain-dumped," recording their conversation along the way. It took five and a half hours, and when they were finished they had a product and a website called www.marketingbraindunp.com.

But according to Alex, they added a twist.

We did three versions.

The bronze version is free. All we have is an email address and name, and they get all five hours of streaming audio, but you can't download it. It's free, but you have to be at your computer to hear it. They're still getting 5 hours of this content, and there were some very, very high-end marketers during this call, so the content is very rich and meaty.

But we have another version called silver. Believe it or not, we only charge $37.00 because we want everyone to get this. It's kind of like a co-branding for Jonathan and me. With that they get the PDF and they get the audio that they can download to their hard drive so that they can listen to it offline.

And the gold version, of course, offers the resell rights. We give them a website, we give them autoresponses for their messages. We teach them how to sell this product to their own constituents so they keep a hundred percent of the product. We call it the 100% commission plan for affiliates.

But here's the part that involves the fax.

When someone buys a silver package, all they've they spent is $37.00.

If we have their fax number, we send them an upgrade reminder. Ten days after they buy, we fax them saying,

'Important upgrade reminder for (their name). As one of our silver members you still have 3 days left to upgrade to Gold and get your three free surprise bonus gifts.'

And there's one of those winky smiles that you do on your keyboard. It says, 'Take advantage of this special offer. Go to our website and click on gold version at the bottom of www.marketingbraindump.com. Your courtesy will be most appreciated. Jonathan and Alex.'

There are less than forty words, and we're not going via autoresponder or email. We're going via fax, and it blows them away. They can't believe they got it by fax. It totally interrupts their pattern, because they know us as Internet marketers, not as brick and mortar marketers.

I do this for my teleclasses that cost $199. There are very specialized ones, like Traffic Conversion Secrets Revealed. I give everyone an auto-reminder the day before, via fax. It's that extra touch.

But the fax is 5 cents; it's nothing. And many times you can do it out of your own fax machine. And if you have like ten upgrades a day, what are ten faxes? Anyone can do it. So the fax is a fantastic tactic to use for upgrades, auto-reminders, or anything dealing with an existing customer when you want to buy more. If you want to have something else to sell to them, just send them a fax and tell them, 'This is it, here's the password, and here's how you get in.' And watch what happens. It's a heck of a lot cheaper than postcards or direct mail. And it will be seen, because generally, your fax machine is right next to your computer.

Also, when that thing is coming through, you hear it come on and you read it. It's not like mail. You read mail typically once a day. I read it three times a week. But faxes you read every single day. It's an exceptional method and I hope everyone uses it.

Who You Should Fax — and Where You Get Their Numbers

As with marketing of any kind, you naturally want to target those who are most likely to be interested in the information you provide in your e-zine.

There are several places you can find them.

You can buy them or rent them. But if you do, make sure they've been recently updated so you're not wasting money on disconnected numbers. There are companies and brokers who provide list buying and renting services. Generally they use SIC (Standard Industrial Classification) codes. You decide which code you'd like to target; they sell you the list. Generally you'll have to pay $50-$100 per thousand.

Generally they'll give you the list as a database, which you then import into your fax software program.

See Appendix C for a list of fax resources.

Is Fax Broadcasting Another Form of Spam?

Some people think so, and they can be very passionate about their beliefs.

There's been some legislation on the subject in recent years, and you should definitely get legal advice on current legislation and regulations.

Here's a website that spells it out for you:

www.fcc.gov/ccb/consumer_news/tcpa.html

Chapter 8
Self-Publishing

Combining their talent and imagination, Mike Litman and Jason Oman conceived of a plan that resulted in a #1 ranking for their book, *Conversations With Millionaires*, on Amazon.com's "Big List."

Even more incredibly, they accomplished that feat in just fifteen hours. At the time, it was a new record for a book achieving #1 status.

Plus, they did it, from start to finish, in 76 days, without

- spending a nickel on advertising
- holding a single book signing
- making a single media appearance to promote the book

Plus, most incredibly of all—*they didn't even write the book!*

Jason Oman is in his late 20s, and he began the path to success when he attended a Tony Robbins seminar at age 17. A self-described "seminar junkie," Jason has been fascinated by successful people, and he became determined to find out how they were able to achieve that success. At age 23, he began a part-time business, and within months he was doing well enough to quit his full-time job and devote himself to his own interests.

After several years of working for himself, Jason began looking around for even more challenges. That was when Mike Litman called him with an idea.

Mike also hasn't even reached his 30th birthday yet. Currently he hosts his own talk show on Long Island, near New York City. He started a marketing company when he was 23, and began helping a family friend with some marketing advice. His friend hosted a small, general interest radio show, and invited Mike on as a guest.

It wasn't long before Mike launched his own radio show on that same Long Island station. He used it as a vehicle to contact people he admired and respected for their success.

Unfortunately, the radio show only lasted a short time before Mike had to give it up for financial reasons. The show wasn't making enough in advertising revenues to sustain itself, so Mike found himself, at age 25, an "ex-talk show host."

Then one day he got a call from Jason.

"Remember all those tapes of interviews you did with successful people,' Jason asked.

Yeah," Mike replied. They're all sitting in a box gathering dust in my parents' basement."

Jason proposed turning the interviews into a book. He reasoned that they could publish it without even having to write anything: they would simply have the interviews transcribed, and then bundle them into a single publication.

Conversations With Millionaires made its debut on early in 2002 and within fifteen hours, it skyrocketed to #1 on the Amazon Big List.

Thanks to their success, Mike has been able to resume his radio show. He buys the time from the station and uses it to pursue his passion — learning everything he can from successful people, whom he interviews regularly.

Mike and Jason emphasize that they owe their real success not to the format or the content, but to their unique marketing formula, which they describe as "loverage." Mike says

> *This specific formula can give you anything you've ever dreamed of. Let me give you a little information about the history of this formula.*
>
> *When we got the idea for the book and started moving forward with it, my network — I mean people I could personally call on for help — was six people. Two of them were my par-*

ents; one was my brother, and three friends. I had nowhere to go.

But what I started to do was to email strangers and create relationships with them. I started going first, so to speak, making contact with people I didn't know, offering to help them in any way that I could.

Six, seven months went by and all of a sudden, I noticed I had developed a network of hundreds of people... maybe even thousands of people, that I had developed a relationship with.

I now believe the biggest currency in business today is not your money. It's your network. Let me say that again. The most important thing in this day and age is the size of your network. As Tim Sanders says in a great book, Love Is The Killer App, 'your network equals your net worth...'

For six or seven months, I was constantly going online, creating new relationships.

In late December 2001, I had all these people who loved me. So Jason and I looked back and found four proven, practical steps that helped us build this huge network and that anyone can use to help them achieve their wildest dreams.

It's all about the concept of 'loverage.'

The name actually came about probably a week or so after we hit number one on Amazon. I was looking for a name that was powerful, and would help people identify with this concept and use this concept in their own life.

So I send out my newsletters normally on Thursday. The night before—actually about 2 o'clock Thursday morning, I was thinking of all these stupid names that were coming to me, and I couldn't think of a good, proper identification for this formula that we'd been developing. So I went to bed a little bit frustrated, and about ninety seconds later the name 'loverage' came to me. Love and leverage together.

Jason says they were especially gratified when their book went to

number one on Amazon, and he credits their use of loverage in making it happen. They had tried to get a number of publishers interested in the concept, but they "laughed at us and said it would never
work."

Next, they decided to start spreading the word about it, trying to
help other people reach their goals and fulfill their dreams. Jason
told us:

> We analyzed what we had done and we started putting
> together a formula, and we created a definition of loverage,
> which is 'using the power of love and leverage to help others
> help you'.
>
> When you think of all the most powerful forces in the uni-
> verse, it's hard to debate that love isn't the most powerful.
>
> Also, you just can't debate the pure, intense power of lever-
> age.
>
> So when you combine the power of love and leverage and
> use them to help others, then by reciprocity people will want
> to help. You can move mountains. You can move the world.
> Miracles can happen for you just like they did for us.

Mike says the loverage formula is one hundred percent foolproof. It
works all the time, and you can look back in thirty, sixty, ninety days
and see your own personal online network exploding.

> You can start taking an hour a day, a few hours a week, and
> start building a network of people that in turn will start help-
> ing you.
>
> There are four steps.
>
> The first step is creating new relationships.
>
> Two, you want to go the extra mile for those relationships.
>
> Three, you want to use the power of asking to manifest op-
> portunities in your life that you can leverage.
>
> And four, you want to take action.

Mike refers to step one of the loverage formula as the real "secret weapon" in the formula.

As I said, you start taking an hour a day, or a couple of hours a week, to start building a network of people that in turn will start helping you.

But how do you do that online? Here's how.

Pick your favorite search engine. Yahoo. Google. It doesn't matter what market you're in. The success market, the gardening market, the craft market.

You do a search for a keyword in your market. And when you get the list of sites that pop up for that key word, you want to go to some of the sites and look at them. And notice if the site owner is doing a good job and putting something of value together.

That's easy. Anybody can do it.

What we did was this. This was the middle of 2001. I would send an email to the owner of that site. I would praise them. I would write, 'Hey Joe, Hey Jennifer! I just came across your site. This is great stuff! This is great information.' Something simple like that. Use exclamation points to get people motivated, to get people excited.

Now let's say you have an Internet newsletter. But you need some way you can promote other people. You want to think: what is your asset of value? What do you have that you can use to provide value to other people?

In your email you want to say, 'I like your site so much I want to promote it in an upcoming newsletter.' You want to look to promote them right there, OR, you want to use this famous line that's been borrowed, imitated and duplicated around the world. You finish your email by saying, 'Joe, Jennifer, Michelle... If I can help you in any way, please let me know.'

You want to end all your emails like that.

Nobody does that! It's so simple, so basic, and yet so power-ful!

You'll find people are going to start emailing you back. You'll start an interaction.

Now a big part of this is your signature file. You want to have a signature file that says who you are. That says what you do. You're not promoting anything, but your signature file will then introduce these people to what you are, what you do. Then they'll check out your site, and then they'll see what you do. And then they'll perceive you as something great, and then you'll start working together, creating relationships.

Jason offers this example.

Put yourself in the shoes of the webmaster, the website own-er out there in cyberspace, and one day, out of the blue, you happen to get an email—from a stranger. Someone they don't even know, who's talking them up saying they're doing a fabulous job, their site's incredible, etc.

Imagine what that person is going to be thinking. They're going to be like 'Wow! I have no idea who the heck this per-son is but I like them already. They believe in what I'm doing. They're willing to help me and be of service to me. They're enthusiastic.'

This is somebody out of the blue that they didn't even know. Bam!

Remember the key: the first impression. You're creating a powerful first impression. The more value, the more service, the more <u>love</u> that you can show them in that first impression, the more magic will happen in the beginning of the relation-ship.

That's what you're really doing. You're creating a magical relationship, right off the bat, by using the power of love. Praise. Enthusiasm. Support. And service.

Mike sets time aside three days a week and focuses on sending out at least five emails. On average, he gets at least eleven or twelve replies per week. The key, he believes, is to give people a chance to feel good about themselves.

We're in a world where we want everything for ourselves. The world is about 'I.' If you've ever read Dale Carnegie you know that people always want to talk about themselves.

But I hear people saying to themselves, 'I don't have time.'

Well, guess what? This is what Jason and I do. We just write one message and then we just cut and paste it to five people. It's the simplest thing.

I write, 'Hey _____.' And then I cut and paste the copy, and I put my signature file on it and I just send it. It will take you five minutes. Maybe just three minutes. Do the search, put out twenty or thirty in a day.

Don't forget. Everybody is all about themselves. Everybody wants to hear themselves talk. What we're doing is we're subjugating our ego. We're coming form the position of give, serve, and love.

Tell them 'I love you.' in a business sense.

The question you need to ask yourself is this. With what I have and what I can do, how can I help this person achieve their goals?

Just as the Bible says, 'As ye sow, so shall ye reap…' You will see amazing things happen.

And you want to give and give and keep giving and giving and going the extra mile for the relationship.

To go to number one on Amazon with the book, Jason and Mike recruited about a dozen people to help them. Everyone did it for free.

Why? Mike explains.

Because of step two. Go the extra mile for the relationship.

When you've already gone the extra mile for somebody else, you tap into reciprocity. They feel an obligation. Whenever

*someone returns one of your emails, start asking yourself,
what can I do for them?*

The key, the key, the key is growing your network.

Jason offers a number of ways to go that extra mile. You can help
someone promote their website, their newsletter, or their products.
And if you really want to make an impression on them, promote
their product without routing sales through your affiliate link.

*In other words, let them keep all the money from the sale
without them paying you a commission.*

*When you tell them you're not going to use an affiliate link,
it makes a huge difference in the impression you're making. When you turn down money and say, 'No, no. I want to
help you pack your pockets with money,' you become like a
superhero. You're not even human. They've never heard this
before. They say, 'Wow! This person is amazing.'*

*This is all setting things up because you're creating a relation-
ship that, by the way, can be a relationship that could last
forever.*

If you've ever heard Mike on the air, you know that his style is very
different. Loud, fast talking, even staccato. He says his delivery
makes him unique among broadcasters, and that's important — not
just on the radio, but also in business.

*Loverage makes you unique. It's so different. Everybody does
the blah-blah thing. I don't care what niche you're in. You're
either unique, or extinct. You need to find ways to be unique,
and you do it by going the extra mile for these people.*

*Jason and I have this network, and 98-99% of these people
we've never met. We've never even talked to them on the
phone. And these people love us. The only reason being…
loverage.*

*When you go the extra mile for people, you don't just win
their minds. What's more important than their minds? You
earn their hearts.*

Always follow through. Always over-deliver. Go way past expectations.

When you turn your mind from taking to sharing, absolute miracles happen.

That's step two of the loverage formula. When you're going the extra mile for the relationship, you go first. You're providing service; you're providing love, without asking anything in return.

Jason and Mike call step three "the power of asking."

According to Mike, this has been called "The Aladdin Factor," after the story of Aladdin and the genie of the lamp. You never know unless you ask.

It's even Biblical. 'Ask and ye shall receive.'

Will everyone say yes?

No. Not everybody will say yes. They key here though is when you come from a position of love, and you ask and somebody says no—you still love them. You're not attached to the end result, because then it would be bribing. Then loverage would be about investing and bribing, which it isn't. It's about giving and about serving. And THEN, there's going to be a time when you use the power of asking.

And when you start asking, because YOU went the extra mile for THEM, people will start coming out of the woodwork, out of the barns, out of the desert, with a smiling stretching from Hawaii to Maine, ready to help. Because you helped them.

And that's when you'll realize that the biggest power in the world is the power of love and the power of leverage, combined together to create the power of loverage.

Because we've followed these steps over time, the people in our network have become salespeople for us.

It all comes back to reciprocity. There's an element of obligation in it. When you start changing your mindset from taking to giving, you'll see miracles happen. But you always have to go first. Always go first.

If you forget about yourself, the world will come storming to your door.

Once you've created the relationship, you've gone the extra mile, and you've used the power of asking, there's one more step.

Once someone says yes, you take immediate action. According to Mike, you jump in and show gratitude.

This is a proven process. It's amazing.

If your network is at a hundred, you need to take it to five hundred. If it's at three, you need to take it to thirty.

The Internet was invented for loverage. You can quickly and easily meet amazing people, and if you use your asset of value—say your newsletter—it doesn't matter if you have three subscribers or three million. Whatever you have. Think creatively and use it to benefit people in your network.

Create the new relationship.

Go the extra mile for the relationship.

Use the power of asking.

Take immediate action.

Do it, and it will result in cash, in riches, in happiness, in success for you and your family.

You can get more detail on how Mike and Jason accomplished their goals by visiting their website at www.amazingbookformula.com

Writing a Book is One Thing, but Getting it Published…

Go to a bookstore and ask one hundred people if they've ever thought about writing a book, and it's likely that each of them would say yes.

But how many of those people would know that they don't need a publisher to do it?

One? Maybe two?

And how much would they be likely to think such self-publication would cost? Ten thousand? Twenty thousand? More?

The truth is, anyone who can write a book can publish it themselves at a cost of less than five thousand dollars.

That comes as a surprise to a lot of people.

But Dan Poynter is the pre-eminent expert in the field of self-published books, and he says awareness of self-publishing has grown considerably in the last few years.

In the early 90s his book, *The Self-Publishing Manual* was only selling at the rate of 3,000 to 4,000 a year. Towards the end of the 90s it was more like 10,000 a year. And now it's up around 16,000 or 17,000 a year. According to Poynter, awareness is growing.

> *I discovered over the last few years that there are a lot of closet writers out there, particularly in minority groups—people who thought that they were shut out of the system. But they wrote and wrote and wrote, never having any hope of being in print. They just wanted to express themselves.*

In *The Self-Publishing Manual* he asked people to send him their books when they finally got it into print and he now gets 10 to 15 books every week. He says the growing numbers lead him to believe that self-publishing is becoming better known. People have begun to realize that there's an alternative—that they don't have to go to a big private New York firm.

He also believes that the average book-buyer doesn't make a distinction between self-published books and one those that are done through a traditional publishing house.

> *People just want to know, 'Is this the information that I'm looking for?' They're trying to solve a problem—maybe they're trying to grow a business or grow their hair or whatever. They're just looking for the book that's going to answer*

*their questions. No one ever asks who the publisher is. Have
you ever heard anybody say, 'Random House? Gee, I love
their books. I buy everything they put out?'*

Dan believes that the published, hard copy book is the foundation of
any information marketer's business. Everything else is built on top
of it.

*For example, sometimes people come to me and they say,
'How can I can get my audio tape my out first? Because I
think I can do that quicker.' And my answer is 'Don't waste
your time. Don't invest your time and money in your audio
products because your audio won't give you as much credibility as a book.*

*Nothing will give you as much credibility as the book. You
can work on a stage play, a calendar, a line of greeting cards,
or workshop. All these things are very nice, but they don't
give you the credibility that the book does.*

*So your book is the foundation. Your seminars, your con-
sulting, your speaking, your special reports, your magazine
articles, everything else is built on top of that and those
often earn more money because now you're a credible person — because you wrote the book.*

There is another advantage to self-publishing: control. According to
Poynter, maintaining control is critical.

*It takes a large publisher 18 months to take your manuscript
and turn it into a product and put it on the shelf. But you can
have your book printed in less than a month. So you're not
going to miss your market, and your information isn't going
to be out of date. Sometimes information is perishable.*

*Furthermore, the big publishers are trying to save money
right now, and they're cutting back on their supplies and
printing on lousy paper and making the type too small. It
makes the book look crummy. People won't buy a crummy
looking book.*

Every book goes through four stages. It has to written, it has to be produced, it has to be distributed, and it has to be promoted. And the big publishers take care of the production and the distribution, but it's up to the author to do the writing and the promotion.

A lot of people don't realize that publishers do not promote books. They won't do anything that will put you in the catalog. And anybody who says I'm getting great support out of my publisher has just started working with that publisher. Anybody who's been with that publisher for a while will tell you, gee, they didn't do anything.

Poynter also believes there's going to be more and more of a demand for self-published books because information is becoming extremely specialized. That makes self-publishing more attractive to prospective authors.

People don't want general information; they want specific information. They don't want a book on how to feel good, they want a book on how to lose weight, getting their hair back, cosmetic surgery, whatever; they want something very specific.

For example, I did books on parachutes and skydiving. I know who my customer is, I know where my customer is and I know what my customer needs. And some big New York publisher wouldn't know any of that. All they know is how to put your book through the bookstore.

As with most things, a lot of the expenses of self-publishing are on the front end. Dan explains:

Let's work on 144 pages, because that's a very economical size and let's talk about a 5 x 8 inch trim size. Initially you'll want to print 500 copies. Most of those go out for reviews and to opinion holders and so on just to get the mine salted—to get the pump primed, so to speak.

Those 500 copies will run you less then $1,500. On top of that you'll probably want to spend another $1,800 on the packaging.

For instance, you need an artist to come up with a cover for this book. And the wrappers are extremely important in the selling of your book.

You also have to set things up so that you'll have a way to ship books. That generates a lot of small expenses: shipping bins, tape and things like that for a small additional cost.

You have to find a place to store your books. You may eventually have three to five thousand of them.

When you print that first 500, and you'll spend about $1,500 on printing. So it costs you $3.00 a piece. But if things go well and you need to go back to print more, they'll drop to a buck at most.

You can see that there's potential to make some pretty good money on that book. Because depending on the type of the book, you're going to be charging anywhere from $12.95 to I'd say, $19.95, so marking it up from a dollar is pretty good.

Once again though, a lot of people don't have much faith in their ability to put words down on paper. They know a lot about their subject, but the physical act of banging out a manuscript intimidates them.

That problem is solved, Poynter says, by hiring a competent editor.

Somebody said years ago that it's much more expensive to try to take ink off paper than it is to put it on. So you want to make sure that the ink that goes on the paper is the correct ink.

Editors not only correct punctuation, grammar, style, but they've got a lot of experience and they pick up other things. I've had my editors say, 'Well now on page 87 you're talking about this, but that's pretty similar to what you said on page 32. Did you mean to repeat yourself?' Oops!

All these people bring a lot extra to your project.

Some charge a lot too. If you just need a little bit of punctuation correction, that's one thing. That's all some editors want to do. Others want to practically rewrite your manuscript.

You should just be sure you're getting an editor who wants to do what you want him or her to do.

It's also helpful that they know something about your subject. That way they can bring a little more content to your manuscript. If you're doing a medical text, get someone who's done medical in the past, somebody who likes it. If you're doing something political and they're in the opposite party, they're not going to be happy campers, you know.

So make sure that they're doing the kind of work that you want. They'll give you a range of prices and depending how much you work, and how long it's going to take, they'll probably charge you by the page or by the hour or by the project.

Just make sure that it's somebody that you want to work with because you're going to be spending a little time with them going back and forth.

Dan offers an entire "Suppliers" section in *The Self-Publishing Manual* and on his website. Besides editors, he offers information about where to get help with other aspects of the book publishing process.

Cover design
This is simply the artwork and print for the front-and-back of the book.

Type settings and layout
These go together. You can set your type yourself but you're going to have to buy a and learn a $700 program. And you're not going to be able get as much out of that program as somebody who uses it all the time. If you hire someone to do the design and typesetting, they'll make sure the chapter headings and subheadings are consistent, the pages are in order, and everything is in the right place. When they're through, all you have to do is send the disk to the printer for printing.

If you're unsure how you want the design and layout to look, Dan suggests going to a bookstore to get a model book. Looks for books in your section. Find a book that you really like—hard cover or soft cover—for color, texture, type style, and size. Buy that book and you use the model. Give it to your designer and to your printer.

Once you've made these choices, and your editing and layout are complete, you can have your book printed in a few weeks. Sometimes it only takes a few days, thanks to digital printing.

With digital, the printer prints with toner on paper as opposed to the traditional books that are done with ink on paper. The result is virtually the same. The big advantage is that there's very little setup time for the digital printer. Basically, you're taking the disk and you're slipping it into their computer.

Fulfillment

This means the physical delivery of hard-copy books to customers. Dan Poynter says it's no big mystery, but some people tend to underestimate what it will cost, whether they do it themselves or farm it out to a fulfillment company.

> The bill will cost 7-14% of your sales and that depends on whether you're shipping wholesale or retail. Obviously if you're shipping wholesale, then they're going out by the carton, and you're expending fewer labor hours per book. But 7% is still a lot of money. You have to buy the shipment bags and cartons to pay for all of this stuff.

> So, one other alternative is to go with a book fulfillment company like 'Book Master' or 'Book Clearinghouse.'

> If you're a person who's constantly on the road because you're, say, a professional speaker, you'll need some kind of back office help. If you don't have anybody at home, then get a fulfillment company and point your toll free number to them. They'll answer the number, take the credit card, and ship the books out. But you'll probably find that it's costing you 25-30% of sales, which is a heck of a lot of money.

> On the other hand you might want to hire somebody to do that shipping for you. It's an ideal job for a high school kid who's otherwise not employable. The kid can come over after school and work for a couple of office shipping books out

*and running to the post office and sort of thing. It's a great
job for a person like that.*

Even if you self-publish, you can still try to get your books into
bookstores and other traditional distribution points. But once again,
you'll generally have to take a lot of time and knock on a lot of doors.
Dan explains:

> *As far as distribution is concerned you get a distributor and
> they have sales reps that go out to the bookstores. The big
> publishers have their own sales reps that go out to the book-
> stores, but all the medium size and small publishers use inde-
> pendent distributors.*
>
> *The good news? There's more room in the bookstores right
> now because the big publishers have been cutting back.
> There's less competition for shelf space then it used to be.*
>
> *Now one thing that you want to be very clear about is that
> when you walk into a bookstore and you see a book in a
> window, or on the end of the aisle—someone's paying
> to put that book there. The bookstore didn't say, 'Oh we
> love this book, we think we'll put it in the window.' A lot of
> people think that the big publishers get the best spots. Well,
> they're paying for those spots. And as a matter of fact, the
> bookstores have even turned down some of the big publish-
> ers.*
>
> *Would you believe that the 'Chicken Soup' books have been
> around for so long, some bookstores got sick and tired of
> them and they didn't want to promote them anymore? It
> didn't matter that the customers liked them just fine, and
> they were still selling well. The bookstores were tired of
> them.*
>
> *Here's the second thing.*
>
> *There's a whole new book model. The whole idea is that you
> can publish 500 books, and in addition to sending them out
> for review, you send them to eight publishers to see if they're
> interested. And if an agent or publisher comes back to you
> with a good offer, then you sell out.*

If no one makes you an offer, it doesn't really matter—you're already off and running and your book is being circulated to reviewers anyway.

So the new book model is really the best approach for everybody. It approaches agents, publishers, reviewers and publicists at the same time. You're not going to be wasting time; you're not going to be waiting for somebody else to get back to you.

Of course, authors now have the option of online distribution companies like Amazon.com. Dan believes these online distributors offer some huge advantages for self-published authors.

Amazon is one of the best things that ever happened to the small press. They have a storefront opened to the entire world 24/7. And they again helped us level the playing field because they want to carry every book. It's not hard to get your book onto Amazon, and even if you don't approach them, eventually they'll find you. They want to carry every book. And they do fulfillment. They have 5 warehouses.

Part 3
Using Low-Cost/High-Return Offline Advertising to Generate Clicks

Chapter 9
Converting Ads to Clicks

Ad Remnants

A few years ago, plenty of people thought classified advertising in broadcast and print media would diminish in favor of online promotion (especially through banners).

But the banner advertising bubble, like the inflated stock prices of Internet start-ups, came crashing down a few months into the new millennium.

Meanwhile, old-fashioned radio, TV, and newspaper advertising has survived, and when you do it well, it can still provide a low-cost promotional vehicle and a decent return on investment, especially if you know some secrets about the business.

PR expert Raleigh Pinskey described three of them recently on our Internet radio show: "remnants, regional buys, and distressed space":

> You know there are deadlines for advertising, to go into a particular issue—lets just say the June issue of a magazine. The deadline for submitting advertising might be May 15. Sometimes though, advertisers pull out at the last minute, or the sales staff doesn't sell all the available space.
>
> So on May 16, you call the advertising department and you say 'Do you have any spaces that aren't filled?' They'll probably sell them for half-price—even less as it gets closer to publication date.
>
> It's like when you go to a fabric store or a carpet store, only

we're talking advertising space instead fabric or carpet. But you can get it for almost nothing. It's wonderful. It's absolutely wonderful.

The other kind is called 'distressed space.' That happens when an advertiser was going to do a big campaign but pulled out because they didn't have any money. So you say they were 'distressed' and that left a big hole in the magazine

And you can get that for a lot less money because they really want to fill that space.

If you call the ad department and say 'Hey, what have you got? Are there any opportunities that I might be able to take advantage of?'

Distressed space is an unusual sort of a thing, so generally you have to get your name on a list. You actually call the advertising people and you say, 'I want to be on the list in case anything falls through. 'And on the 15th if you don't sell anything, I want to be on the list.

Of course, that means you don't know if you're going to be in that issue or not. But if you don't care, or if it's not timely, then you have some great opportunities to get cheap advertising through remnants and distressed space.

Raleigh says there's another insider strategy most people don't know about: regional ads in national magazines.

You can be in People Magazine, in a full-page ad, for very little money, in your own region. In other words, you don't have to buy national.

Let's just say that you only want to advertise to people in your city or maybe state. Maybe you're doing a concert or maybe you're having a sale at a certain store. So you can take out regional advertising as opposed to buying the whole magazines. And it's pennies compared to what people think they would have to pay to get in a major magazine. It's affordable; and even better, it's more targeted.

Just call up the ad rep and say you want to do a regional buy.

Raleigh knows what she's talking about. Her clients have included stars like Paul McCartney, Sting, Blondie, David Bowie, John Lee Hooker, Herbie Mann, and dozens of companies both large and small. She also authored one of the "Chicken Soup for the Soul" series.

Visit Raleigh's sites by clicking on www.get-free-publicity.com/rpinskey.html

David Frey of www.marketingbestpractices.com has used a number of ads successfully in several different industries. Recently he consented to be interviewed by phone, and he shared some of his most successful techniques.

Lead-generation Ads

If you want to sell a product, the fastest way to get the word out is usually advertising.

But you can also use advertising to find prospects that will buy from you in the future—as they move through your profit pipeline.

In that case, you use advertising to get them into the profit pipeline.

The sales tool in this case, is a "lead-generation ad."

Now most niche marketers have used this same strategy for years, and it has worked for years. It's proven, and it's simple.

It's a multi-media approach because you combine some type of offline advertising with a toll-free recorded telephone message system.

Both www.automatedmarketingsystem.com and www.patlive.com offer these systems.

David Frey of www.marketingbestpractices.com in Houston, Texas, has enjoyed a lot of success using this technique.

> The lead-generation ad, first of all, has to have a compelling headline—a very compelling headline that gets the attention of your target market.
>
> For instance, if you want to capture an accountant's attention, then you need to have a word in there that saying something

like 'Accountants,' or 'Warning Accountants' or 'Attention Accountants in the city of Houston.'

The headline is the sifting system, and it needs to be compelling. If it's not, this whole strategy will fall on its face.

The second thing is you offer some type of special report. Now that special report could be in audiocassette form, it could be in a CD and it could be in just regular paper. I've done all three. In fact the audiocassette has gotten me the biggest response rate of all of them. And it was simple to do. I just sat at my table and wrote an article and I talked into the audiocassette recorder. And that's it. And I snazzed it up a little by going to www.musicbakery.com and put a little bit music at the beginning and a little bit of music at the end.

Then I offered the cassette in a lead generating ad.

Now, I'll give you 3 different examples and then I'll give you an actual real live example from the industry that I market to.

The first place I do my own ads is in trade magazines. So if you're in niche marketing in a specific industry the first place you want to go is to those trade magazines and usually all of the trade magazines have a back section of the magazine called the 'Market Place.' That's where they put all the small classified ads.

If you were going after the general public, you'd want to do it in the newspaper. And I would certainly recommend that you do it in a small local newspaper before you would do it in a major newspaper. Here in Houston, I would do it to maybe one of the local advertising newspapers. They have a weekly newspaper that comes out every Wednesday. I put a very large ad in it and it only cost me about $300 to reach 45,000 people.

The free audiocassette offer got a great response. And because of that, I was able to put a smaller ad in the Houston Chronicle. Now the Houston Chronicle cost me a whole lot more, but their circulation is up near a million I believe.

When you do this you always want to remember one key metric: CPM. CPM stands for costs per thousand. And you always want to do a CPM calculation when you go to do print ads.

For instance, my local ad was 45,000 people and it cost me $300. So I take the $300 and divide it by the 40,000 and then by 40. That gives me my cost per thousand. I do a similar calculation for the Houston Chronicle.

Now, I always asked to put the ad up in the upper right-hand part of the paper. Now they never guarantee you a spot, but I always tell them that if this is a test ad, and if it's successful, I going to run this puppy for a long time. So they'll usually help me make it successful by putting it in the upper right hand part of the paper. That's what most people look at first.

That's a little counter-intuitive to most people because they've always heard that everyone reads from left to right... That's true when they read a line, but when you open a newspaper, your eye automatically goes to the upper right hand side, so that's where you want to try to place your ad.

And I would always ask for some type of discount. I would always tell them it was a test, and then I'd ask if they have some kind of discount for a direct marketing test. I'd also ask if they have a discount for frequency, or a 'frequency rate.'

Don't just take a regular CPM they'll offer you. You should never pay the list rate.

So getting those nuts and bolts out of the way, let me give you some different examples.

Lets suppose you were a financial planner. If you were a financial planner you can offer a special report called '10 Simple Ways to Protect Your Hard-Earned Assets.' That would be a good special report for the senior industry. Because when you're young you're interested in making money, when you're older you're interested in protecting your money and making it work well for you.

I could even make the title much stronger. I would put 'Senior Adults: Learn 10 Simple Ways to Protect Your Hard Earned Assets.' And I would put the words 'senior adults' in big letters.

For a chiropractor I would put, 'How To Naturally Stop Lower-Back Pain Without the Use of Drugs.' The people who respond to that are the types of people are going to use a chiropractor, because those people who respond to that are probably not going to want to use drugs and that's what chiropractors are all about.

It's important to use psychology in your offer because it will absolutely determine how many leads or how many email addresses you get.

Let's say you are a travel company. You could offer a report called '11 Little Known Luxurious Hide-a-ways That Won't Break the Bank.'

A lot of people don't want to fly right now, so you could also say '11 Luxurious Hide-A-Ways Within Driving Distance That Won't Break The Bank.'

Anyway, those are some different titles you can use. The title is so important, because that has a lot to do with how many leads you are going to get.

Now here's the last example

I had niche-marketed to the pool and spa industry. So I did an ad for a client offering a special report. The ad is just a little 2 x 2 square. The headline takes up about 20% of the top of that ad. And it says,

'Hot Tub Buying Mistakes Can Cost you Money.'

You put a dash, and then comes the body of the ad. It reads,

'More Americans than ever are purchasing hot tubs to ease stress, back pain, and improve their sleep. However, many hot tub shoppers quickly realize that buying a hot tub can be a confusing process. A wrong decision cannot only cost you money but a lot of frustration and heartache. Before you pur-

chase your hot tub, you should read a recently released special report titled, 'Seven Deadly Hot Tub Purchasing Mistakes', listing the common mistakes buyers make when purchasing a hot tub. To receive your free special report, call 1-800, ***-**** ext 7, 24hrs for a free recorded message. This report is free and so is the call.'

I've had a lot of my clients use this, and they have reported just an incredible result just from this small ad. Anyone can do the same thing.

Okay. Now when those people respond to the ad they'll call up the 1-800 number. I like to use www.automaticmarketing solutions.com because they give me 100 different extensions. That's nice because I can have 5 different ads. It gives me the ability to track where the leads come from.

For example, I can have an offer for a free report on my business cards, on the referral cards, and I can be advertising in 2 newspapers. I can also be sending out a newsletter. Each has a different extension so I know exactly what return I'm getting for the dollar that I'm spending.

And in each one of those I'm offering a free report to start a lead-generation program or sequential mail marketing program to them. Because I can use an extension on each one of the telephone numbers. That's so important when you do offline lead-generation.

Now once you've got them on the phone, then you want to sell again, because in lead-generation you always have to sell the next step. You're not trying to sell them the final product. You're just trying to sell the next step.

For instance, this would be the intro script.

'Hello and thank you for calling your 24-hour consumer information line. Please enter your one digit extension now.'

And they enter that one digit extension, and they hear another recorded message.

'Hello and thank you for requesting this special report entitled

'Seven Deadly Spa Purchasing Mistakes...' Shopping for a spa can be a confusing task and a wrong decision can cause a lot of headache and disappointment... not to mention a lot of money. This special report will give you the insider informa- tion you need to ask smart questions to get the spa you want at the right price. To receive your free report leave your name and address at the end of this message and I'll send it right out for you. Please speak slowly and spell any uncommon names so that we'll get your mailing information correct. Oh and by the way, as a special bonus I would like to email you a valuable free e-book titled 'The Spa Buyer Consumer Infor- mation Guide,' which answers many of the frequently asked questions that spa buyers have. So please leave your email address as well so that I can send you this special gift. Make sure to spell your email address so that you can get it correct. Thank you for calling this free consumer information line and again, leave your name, your address and email address at the end of this message and I'll get your free information out to you right away.'

My clients and I experience an 85% lead rate off this script. 85% of the people leave an email address. It's phenomenal. A very quick way to build leads.

Using Ads for Surveys

What's one of the best ways to use ads?

As surveys.

Alex Mandossian says this is how to conduct an online survey in any publication.

Here's one I saw from Inc. magazine. It says,

'We want your opinion.' That headline should say, 'We need your advice.' Remember, I've tested 'advice' and 'opinion' over and over and over again, and the word 'advice' gets a better response. And people are willing to give advice.

Asking for advice also says to the reader, 'I know I could be doing better, and I'd like you to tell me how.' There are some embedded commands there that are very, very powerful.

Anyway, the body of the ad says

'Join the Inc. leadership forum. Participate in brief online polls that match your interests. Share your business challenges and successes. Help shape our future editorial focus.' So basically, they're saying, just give us your opinion and you'll help shape this magazine.'

Which is very smart. Then it says,

'Join now (so it's a membership) by visiting www.inc.com/ panel.'

No phone number. It's a full-page ad and it's just for getting an opinion in an e-poll.

The best way to get a response is to ask for advice. Don't sell something. Get their opinion. That's the best way to be market-centric. Ask them what they're looking for and then give it to them.

They'll usually give you their name and number, or at least an email address. You send them a thank you, and then at some point in the future, you offer them a product.

So a space ad is a great way to collect email addresses. It's not for everybody, because it's costly, but it certainly is an effective way to do a survey and have get people to go directly online

Buying Lists of Subscribers

If you've published an e-zine for more than a few minutes, you probably know about co-registration.

This is a process where someone signs up for a free prize, a program, or even another e-zine. Before they can click away, they're presented with a list of similar publications they may be interested in. All they have to do, usually, is click on a check box and hit send. They're automatically subscribed to the publications they checked.

If you use a co-registration service, you generally pay anywhere from ten to fifty cents per subscriber.

Some people have used these services to build huge lists very quickly.

What many online publishers don't know is this: there are offline lists you can buy also.

Spamming is always a concern of course, and you should be careful to make sure you're dealing with a reputable company and that your list is indeed targeted.

But there are also ways you can acquire those lists at virtually no cost. David Frey describes one technique he used to get 6500 subscribers for "free" from a trade magazine.

I've used it multiple times and it works. I niche-market to the CPA industry and I wanted to buy a list so that I could start a direct mailing list. To buy a list that you can use over and over within a 12-month period usually costs about $.25 per name. You can rent the name for about $.10 per name, but then you can only use it one time. But to get a list you can use multiple times it's about $.25.

So I wanted to get a list that was about 7000 people. That's $1750.00.

But before I bought those names I called up a trade magazine and said 'You know, I'm doing a lead generation marketing test and I have 2 choices. I went out and talked to some mailing list brokers and they offered me a list of 7,000 names for $1750 and I can use them multiple times. My other choice is do a significant ad in your trade magazine.'

And then I said, 'If I buy the list for $1750, I know that I'm going to get 7,000 addresses. But if I spent $1750 with you Mr. Trade Magazine, I'm taking a chance on how many leads I'm going to get. The leads are probably going to be better but I might get a fraction, just a fraction of the 7,000.

Would you be interested if I bought a display ad in your trade magazine, would you share 7,000 addresses with me from your list?'

I made the same offer to two publications. One took me up on it and the other didn't.

But here's the really great part. When they sent it to me, 3200 of the names included email addresses. Now what would it cost to get 3200 email addresses in your niche market? And how would you even get it? You would have to do display ads from here to next year to do it.

This way, I got a big display ad, and I got the 7,000 names and I had an instant mailing list for emails.

And so if you're target marketing to trade magazines, or niche magazines, ask to see if they'll share their mailing list as a bonus for buying ads. If they will, ask them if they'll please include the phone numbers and email addresses.

I'll tell you—all the magazines collect email addresses. So I amassed my list very quickly that way.

On-site and In-store Promotions

If you own or operate a brick and mortar business, you have numerous possibilities for gathering email address and interacting with your customers.

In her excellent book, How To Promote Your Local Business on the Internet, www.get-free-publicity.com/bizpromo.html, Sharon Fling recommends the following ideas.

Fishing for Customers

Here's an easy way of finding out who your customers are: offer a business card drawing when they visit your store. Put a spiffy-looking fishbowl on your counter and anyone who comes into your business can put in a business card for a chance to win a prize. Ask for their email address so you can notify the winner by email.

Coupons

Give out coupons for discounts on free merchandise—in exchange for their email address; you should also utilize coupons in your on-line campaign. A recent survey (March, 2001) showed that 55% of customers prefer coupon delivery via email, versus only 29% that prefer to receive newspaper coupons.

As a variation of this, you can print up "bag-stuffers" offering special incentives to people who go to your website. Bag-stuffers are simply small flyers you put in the bags along with your merchandise that they take with them when they leave your store.

If your business doesn't lend itself to this technique, you can always hand the flyers to departing customers with their receipt. Train employees to point out the value the customer receives with the receipt.

Contests

Remember those contests where customers have to guess how many marbles are in a jar? People love those. Whatever your line of business, there's got to be a contest you can come up with featuring one of your items. Or you could have a drawing where people have to give their name and email address to enter. Everyone is notified by email of the results, and maybe given an extra discount on their next purchase.

Computer Demo

Set up a computer in your store with your website displayed on the screen. Invite customers to come and click around, and offer a prize or discount on their next purchase if they input their email address.

Giveaways

Give away free samples or promotional items with your business address inscribed, including URL and email address. They can range from a few cents each to several dollars each, depending on your budget—T-shirts and caps, pens, calendars, playing cards and CD holders.

Demonstrations

This is a way to attract people to your business and show them how to use your products, as well as establish your credibility. For example, cooking shows, painting demos and art exhibits can all work well, and are good opportunities to collect email addresses in exchange for discount coupons.

Window Display

Put your URL in your window or somewhere that it's visible from the outside. You can use that static cling stuff.

Ask

When someone buys from you, ask for their address at a cash register so that you can send them discount coupons and notify them of special promotions and sales.

Voice mail/answering machine message

Always include your URL at the end of any answering machine or voice mail message, directing customers to the website for more information, including store hours, directions, your catalog, etc. When ending a conversation with customers, remind them to check the website for the latest specials and discounts.

Local events

Local events are great opportunities for generating publicity. Rent a booth, and distribute flyers and giveaways. Sponsor a local event. Try to tie into your business and post it on the website.

Put information about local events on your website, but *only* if you update the site on a regular basis. There's nothing worse than seeing an announcement of an event that happened 6 months ago.

Another idea is to include a message board where people can exchange ideas and information. People want to feel a sense of community, and if that happens on your website then you'll generate a lot of goodwill.

If you have the time, you may want to offer your services to nonprofit organizations, especially if doing so will attract your target audience. Getting involved with the community is always a good idea—it's a way to give back, and you'll make contacts that could lead to more business.

For more depth on this topic, get *How to Plan and Promote Sizzling Special Events* by Joan Stewart and Debra J. Schmidt.

Joan and Debra have created six audiocassettes and a collection of 15 valuable checklists that show you in step-by-step detail how to make your next event a smashing success. That's 847 tips! See what's included in this package and download three of their checklists for free. Go to www.get-free-publicity.com/publicityhound.html for more information.

Also see Chapter 13, "How To Do Well By Doing Good".

Part 4
Offline Networking

Chapter 10
Marketing Through Seminars and Public Appearances

Tom Wood is a professional speaker and network marketer who delivered an interesting, extremely insightful presentation at a recent Mark Joyner seminar we attended.

"You don't just want customers," Tom said. "You want missionaries. People who are willing to go out and tell the world about you, without being asked."

But how do you convert browsers into buyers, buyers into customers, and customers into missionaries?

Tom described the process using the following graph.

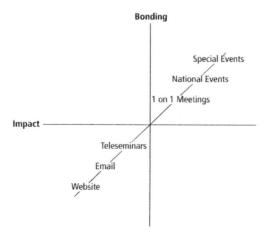

Isn't it interesting that so many Internet marketers focus hours and hours of attention on their website and email strategies, while completely ignoring "bricks" like teleseminars, one-on-one meetings, workshops and big national events like Mark Joyner's?

Our friend George Callens www.cyberdell.com and www.profession alinternetmarketer.com says

> Some people think the Internet is a means to get rich while withdrawing from society.
>
> Nothing could be further from the truth.
>
> The Internet is a means to interact with people and societies around the entire globe! This interaction must be sustained with continued, direct contact, even though it's via email.
>
> To truly leverage this relation-building tool (the Internet) you must develop a subset of personal face-to-face relationships with the key movers and shakers in your particular industry.
>
> I only know of one effective, economical way to do this — attend live trainings, seminars, and workshops that relate to your particular industry.
>
> I attend the live events as often as I can. Three carefully planned days at one of these live events will fast forward your business by one year.

George offers an audiocassette course on how to get maximum mileage out of every live event you attend. www.cyberdell.com

Alexandria K. Brown, who's known around the Internet as "The E-zine Queen" www.get-free-publicity.com/eq.htm added these thoughts when we interviewed her recently on our radio show.

> Some people ask me, 'If you're the E-zine Queen, why is so important to take three days out of your schedule to go hear a succession of speakers talking and talking and talking?' Well, in fact I think going to seminars and workshops pays huge dividends on the time you invest in them.
>
> First of all, it's really important to surround yourself with peo-

ple who are both positive and successful. You get so pumped up with new ideas and energy.

But there's something even more important than the content and motivation. I'm talking about the connections you make. When you meet someone in person, you feel a hundred times more connected to him or her. You can build relationships much faster and even form partnerships that would take you much, much longer just through email. And those relationships and partnerships can open doors that just wouldn't be possible otherwise.

There are also some spectacular opportunities to grow your opt-in list. Let's talk about some of those.

Maximizing Live Events When You're an Attendee

Postcards

We talked a lot about how to use postcards earlier in the book. Here's how to use them when you're attending a seminar or workshop.

Bring an ample supply of your personal postcards with you. These are preferably webcards—in other words, snapshots of your website printed in postcard form.

You can write part of your cards in advance, leaving blanks to fill in later on. This is where you'd put something slightly personal—perhaps a reflection back to something you talked about when you met. You can then write in something like

> My phone number is 1-877-232-4002 and I have a free e-course on how to "How To Triple Your Opt-in List and Double Your Online Profits In Half the Time."

But here's the thing most people never think of.

You put a special URL on the card, like www.masterlistbuilder.com/free-pc.

The special URL tells you the person joined your list through a postcard they got at the seminar.

Now you can put them on a separate sub-list of people who attend seminars. Next time you're promoting someone else's seminar, or doing one yourself, you make sure to contact everyone on that sub-list. If they've paid to go to one seminar, they might be inclined to pay to go to another one.

So you've not only captured a subscriber, but you've captured someone you know is a targeted prospect for seminars.

There's another kind of postcard you can use in situations like this. Again, it has a picture of your website, but here's the difference.

This postcard contains a pre-printed offer to sign up for your newsletter, program, seminar, or whatever.

One of the most powerful techniques involves a digital camera.

Get pictures of yourself with other attendees. You can even get pictures of yourself with some of the speakers.

After the event, send them an email or a postcard saying, "Hey I have a picture of us, or I have a picture of us on the website and here's the website address."

You can almost bet they'll go to the website to see their picture.

Now, to see their picture, they have to click on a banner on that special page. Not just any banner, either. One of your promotional banners.

When they click on the banner, they're re-directed automatically to your main website, where they're greeted by a pop-up inviting them to subscribe to your newsletter.

If you feel comfortable shortening the process a little, you can also just put a pop-up on the site where their picture is posted. But when they go to the site, they're presented with a pop-up recruiting them to become a subscriber.

BCCDs, or Business Card CDs

"That's really neat..."

"What a great marketing gimmick..."

"Does it work like a regular CD?"

Those are just some of the comments we heard at several recent seminars when we started passing around our "BCCD."

That's "Business Card Compact Disc."

BCCDs are real, working CDs shaped like business cards.

"Most people don't realize that a CD can be produced in any shape you want," says Ten Cadle of Avalon Multimedia in San Antonio www.littledisc.com "They don't have to be round."

You can put about eighty megabytes of digital information on a BCCD. That's about an eighth of a regular sized disc—still a ton of information.

Some people even put audio and video on them.

We put three sample chapters of this book, a table of contents, and a free e-book on the one we were passing around. It caused quite a stir. Most people had never seen anything like it before.

We liked them for a couple of reasons.

There was the curiosity factor, of course. It was a real attention-getter.

But we also used it to recruit subscribers for our lists. When they popped the BCCDs into their player, the web page we created for this book appeared. Naturally, a pop-up also appeared offering some free reports if they signed up for our newsletters.

Everything else on the BCCD was in effect, in e-book format.

We used Armand Morin's ebookgenerator program, at www.get-free-publicity.com/ebookgenerator.htm to produce the e-books.

Our webmaster, Tim Flor, gave us a couple of lines of code so the e-book would open automatically when someone placed it in their CD tray.

The blank CDs are available in a number of places. We got ours from Polyline Corporation www.polylinecorp.com. They cost about fifty cents each. Add another dime for the plastic sleeve that protects them, and about half-a-penny for a label.

We did the labels ourselves in Microsoft Publisher, and burned the CDs in a regular CD burner.

You can also order the labels and the plastic sleeves from Polyline.

There's one thing that's dangerous about these odd-shaped CDs however. They can only be used in a tray-style CD player. If you try to run them in a car CD player, or in one of the increasingly popular computer "slot" players — they won't work.

Not only won't they work, they might jam or even damage the player.

So, if you decide to use them, be sure to put a plainly visible disclaimer on the label. And warn as many people as you can in person.

If they're used correctly, though, they're wonderful, attention-grabbing little gizmos.

Handouts at Seminars and Public Appearances

Can you get any more brick and mortar than physically handing something out to somebody? But how do you use the handout to build your subscriber base? Once again, Alex Mandossian has some tips.

> *I use handouts to boost online sales at seminars, at book signings, anything physical.*
>
> *I have a handout that also doubles as a postcard. It tells the full postcard story. It has testimonials. It also has my offer. It has the cover of the book and the CD-ROM that you get with the book. I use this as a handout when I go to a seminar, and instead of bragging about the book and how great it is, I use it as my business card. It also includes my phone number, it has my website address, it has everything on it.*
>
> *So if you're going to give a handout at a seminar, make it worthwhile. Make it an offer. If you just have business cards, you can list the benefits of your website on the back of the card. Or you can put an offer of some kind on it. Something like 'To learn how to become a world-class copywriter for under $80 visit www.copywritingcoach.com.'*

And don't just put www.copywritingcoach.com there. Spell out the benefit.

And that can be a handout.

Here's another idea.

Bob Berg is a dear friend of mine and also the author of End-less Referrals and Winning Without Intimidation. He's also written a book about gossip. He's a fantastic, fantastic writer and author, just a heck of a guy. We both use this technique.

When we attend a conference, we have these postcards that have our name and picture on them. They're pre-printed and there's a little space for a handwritten note. And we have first-class stamps on them.

J. Conrad Levinson, who lives in my hometown here in San Rafael and is also one of my mentors, says that 68% of all sales are lost because of a lack of follow-up. I personally believe that after a seminar, because you get overwhelmed and you come back with a stack of business cards, you need at least 10-20 days to get back to everyone. You'd like to get back to them immediately, but you never do.

Furthermore, I believe you lose 10% in memory and interest every single day. So after day 10, you're looking at the card and you're asking yourself 'Who was that again?' You lose some of the flavor, magic and nuance that you had at the seminar.

I write a handwritten note to everyone I meet, even if I'm a speaker. And I put something in it from the conversation we had. I mail the postcard right at the hotel where the event is held, so in a day or two they're going to get a postcard, handwritten from me, mailed right from the seminar location.

That's a great brick and mortar follow-up. But I don't stop there.

I'm going to tell them, 'How would you like to get 3 free chapters of 'How to Market with Postcards?' On me! I give them the website. They go to the website and they down-load the chapters, and 7 out of 100 will purchase it if they go into my autoresponder series, which is very, very high for an autoresponder series.

You can have web cards printed locally, or you can go to www.web-cards.com, give them your URL, and they'll print them up for you. When you order in bulk, the cards only cost a few cents each.

Generating Subscribers When You're a Speaker or Seminar Leader

We have a friend who says, "Would you rather sell to one person, or a roomful of people?"

When you're invited to speak at a seminar or workshop, you not only get a room full of people, you get a room full of pre-heated prospects.

There's another important point to keep in mind.

You've probably heard that you need anywhere between seven and twenty-seven contacts with a prospect before they'll trust you enough to punch their credit card numbers onto your website sales form.

In a seminar, all you need is one. By being on stage, you get immediate credibility no amount of web copy, no matter how well written, can buy. It can shorten the sales cycle enormously.

If you're smart though, you don't take that gift for granted. There are still a number of strategies, tactics and techniques you can use to make sure those people in the audience get more than one opportunity to buy from you.

Use some of the following ideas to turn those seminar attendees into lifetime customers.

Use a carefully constructed PowerPoint presentation

Some professional speakers avoid using PowerPoint or other presentation software because they feel it's better to keep the audience's attention focused completely on them.

For list-building purposes though, using PowerPoint helps brand you—and it helps get people to your sign up form.

Every page of your presentation should start with a banner or a graphic that mirrors your website. It's subliminal branding. You should also include your "USP" or Unique Selling Position: somewhere on the screen. For instance: "No Nonsense Guide For Newbie Netpreneurs."

Follow that with your actual URL and the subscribe link.

If you can squeeze your signature file on the screen without cluttering it, do that too.

Every page of your PowerPoint presentation should contain those items if possible.

Do that and you won't even have to sell from the stage. Your PowerPoint presentation will be doing it for you—and the audience probably won't even realize it.

Offer your audience a copy of your outline
We're using the same principle here as we mentioned in the section on teleseminars.

Most people take notes during a seminar or workshop, but will jump at an offer to get you're a printed, neatly organized outline to go with them.

Tell them several times during your presentation that they can go to a special web page to get a copy of your outline. When they arrive at that page, of course, the first thing they see is an invitation to subscribe to your newsletter. Once they subscribe, they're directed to a special web page that contains your material.

You can also set it up so they go on a sub-list ONLY for people who attended that particular seminar. That way, you can do some specialized, targeted follow-up through your sub-list.

Now, you also make sure to put a link back to your main site. So anyone who hasn't subscribed already will get another invitation if they click to your home page.

Once again, you're just giving people more and more reasons to visit your website, and more and more opportunities to subscribe.

"Back of the Room" Tactics

Most of the time, speakers are allowed to set up a table in the back of the room to sell products. Usually, they either stack their business cards in one neat pile, or they don't put any business cards on the table at all.

We recommend spreading out your business cards neatly toward the front of the table. Just one or two rows, maybe fifteen to twenty cards at a time.

This makes a stronger visual impression, and also makes it harder for them to overlook your cards. They're more likely to pick up a card from an "array" like this than a single stack that they might not even see.

One warning though. Don't place the cards to neatly in rows and columns. People won't want to pick up a card because they'll be afraid to 'ruin the display." Cards that are arranged too neatly say, in a non-verbal way, "Look but don't touch." You want them to touch. In fact, you want them to take.

Here's another trick.

Remember we said that it helps to have something written on both sides of the card?

Place some of your cards front side up, and some with the back side up. That way, people will just naturally take a moment to figure out which side is which, and also make sure they're not looking at two completely different cards.

You've just gotten them to pay closer attention to your material. And that's what you want them to do, right.

We attracted a huge amount of attention at several recent seminars by placing our "BCCD" on the table where we had set up our radio show recording equipment. People really inspected them closely. At least a dozen people asked us "What do these cost?"

When they're asking question like that, you know you've been noticed.

Take Pictures
We covered "digital camera tactics" earlier, so we won't repeat them here.

Except to say this.

When you're a speaker at an event, and you ask people you've never met—"ordinary attendees" from the audience—to have a picture taken with you, the impact on them is enormous.

They think, "Wow, this 'guru' wants to take a picture with me." It just blows people away—and bonds them to you in a manner that's just about impossible to overstate.

Follow all the same strategies we mentioned previously.

Invite Attendees To Dinner
If attendees are "wowed" when you have your picture taken with them, how do you think they'll feel if you invite them to have lunch or dinner with you?

And you buy.

You've probably just made a friend for life—and a customer for life too.

Remember what Frank Garon said? You bond to people by showing them that you're real, by breaking bread with them.

We recommend groups of four to six for lunch. You can invite eight-to-ten for dinner. That way everyone is within earshot, and you can manage group dynamics more easily.

Make small talk for a while, and then ask each person to introduce himself or herself, describe their business, and mention their URLs.

After they've done that, ask each to talk about the biggest challenge they face in growing their business. After they describe it, you can ask other people around the table to offer feedback and advice.

You act as moderator, which automatically puts you in an elevated psychological position. They already consider you an expert because you're a speaker. Doing this raises you even high in their estimation.

Will it cost you some money? Of course.

Will you gain subscribers and probably even lifetime customers as a result?

Absolutely.

In fact you'll probably recoup the cost of the lunch or dinner many times over through sales, word of mouth and goodwill.

Don't think of it as an expense. Think of it as an investment.

An investment that will pay dividends over and over in years to come.

How to Get Traffic and Subscriptions from People Who Don't Even Attend Your Seminar

Unless you operate a full-time speaking/publishing machine like Tony Robbins or Zig Ziglar, marketing yourself through seminars may seem like the slow way to go in building your email list.

Most people would have to spend a lot of time and money promoting the seminar, and only a few people might show up.

It hardly seems worth the effort.

But there are several ways you can use seminars as a vehicle to get the attention of hundreds — maybe even thousands — of prospects in your target market. Once you've got that attention, you can lead them to your subscription page and sign them up for your list, even if they never attend a single seminar you're promoting.

Raleigh Pinskey shared this tactic with us. In this instance, she was speaking to an estate-planning consultant, but the principles she describes would work for just about anyone.

> I've consulted with a lot of financial planners over the years, and have several clients...
>
> Why not approach a local BMW dealership, for example, and ask them if they'd like to 'sponsor' your event. And then use

their mailing list. Have them mail it out. Do things like that. Find that age group—that yuppie age group that's sandwiched in, and is about to put their parents into long-term care. Look at all the estate planning that goes with that, the power of attorney and the will and stuff, and whatever.

So I would try to find that age group, and maybe not so much the age group as the occupation group, and ask them if they want to sponsor your conference or your seminar.

Now, you can't just ask the dealership or list owner of the email addresses of their clients and then start sending them offers. That's spamming.

But by getting them to mention you, your services, and your URL, you can get people visiting your site and checking you out.

That, of course, gives you an opportunity to persuade them to opt into your list.

Chapter 11

Joint Ventures with Offline Businesses

Did you notice that about ten years ago, you started seeing, for instance, Subway restaurants in gas stations? Or McDonald's in supermarkets? Or Wendy's in truck-stops?

These combinations were called "strategic alliances." You could also call them joint ventures.

And if it made sense for Subway, McDonald's, and Wendy's, you can be pretty sure the same principle will work for you to help build your list.

David Frey of www.marketingbestpractices.com has used offline joint ventures repeatedly.

> One way is to approach a business and offer to do a joint venture in which they put a fish bowl or some type of bowl out of their cashier desk that people can throw their business cards into.
>
> For instance, go to a restaurant and tell them, 'We'll put this bowl out. You'll do a drawing to give away a free dinner or free lunch on a monthly or weekly basis.'
>
> So the business people will throw their cards in exchange for entrance into the free drawing. And then at the end of the week they draw the cards.
>
> Here's what you do that gives them the incentive to give away a free meal.
>
> You enter those cards into a database and to do an emailing

for them. You can enter the names manually, of course, but you can also buy a reader to run the cards through. It'll create the database automatically.

You have to make it clear to your joint venture partner that you own the list. Offer them a copy if they want it, but emphasize to them that the list is yours.

David says you can also use the same principle to drive people to your website and collect their email address through a checkbox or popup.

Microsoft and Taco Bell did this very successfully. Taco Bell wanted to introduce their Quesadilla. Microsoft wanted to introduce their XBox. Both of their products were coming out at the same time. So the Microsoft guys went to Taco Bell and said, 'Listen for every Quesadilla that you sell why don't you give them this ticket. It's a ticket for a free drawing giveaway to get a free XBox.'

And of course, the demographics matched up perfectly because the people who ordered a Quesadilla were the people who would want an XBox.

And so when you went to buy a kids meal you'd get this ticket. It gave you explicit instructions. Go home, get on the Internet, type in Xbox.com, and then follow the directions on the Internet to sign up for the free drawing.

I did it myself. And they not only got my email address, but they got my mailing address and my demographic information.

I checked that site. They had hundreds of thousands of people. Hundreds of thousands. They had one of the largest and most successful rollouts of any of their products with XBox.

Keep in mind, Microsoft is a software company. They were competing against Nintendo and Sega. And that's how XBox entered the market. It was a juggernaut.

Incentive Packages

We've all seen entry boxes in restaurants, convenience stores, or other high traffic businesses which offer you a free vacation, heath club membership, etc. when you drop in a registration card.

Some of these have gotten a bad name in recent years because phone companies have used them as a ploy to get you to switch long distance companies. If you didn't read the fine print on the back, you started getting bills from someone you never heard of.

Nonetheless, offers like free vacations and other incentives still work, and you can legitimately use them to get people to subscribe to your list or visit your site.

There are a variety of packages, and of course, there's a catch. Yes, you get an unbelievable deal on lodging at a far away destination. No, you don't get airfare as part of the package.

Plenty of people take the deal, even though most never take the vacation.

David Frey has also used this kind of incentive in his niche market.

In the pool & spa business, I would go right over to a health club and I'll say to the health club 'Would you like to give away a free vacation to your customers as a way to say thank you? Let me show a way to do it. There's no cost in it for you at all. Plus I'll build you a mailing list. '

So they give away the voucher, and the voucher requires them to go to a specific page on your website. But to get to the correct page, they have to go through your front page. That gives you a chance to capture the email addresses.

Here's another way I've seen this done.

I went into OfficeMax just the other day and they had a briefcase on display. A nice leather briefcase and it was open. In front it said, 'Do you want this briefcase?' And it had a bunch of business cards there. And it said throw your business card in.

And so people just walked by it and tossed their business

cards in and voila! They started to create a customer database.

Jim Erskine wrote a book called Email Profits, detailing how he has used this strategy to amass a huge database. Jim has joint ventures with dozens of restaurants. He then offers the list to other local merchants.

Suppose you ran an accounting practice. What accountant wouldn't want to send an email to 30,000 business people right there in his or her neighborhood? Most people wouldn't even know where to go to look for a list so geographically targeted.

It will take a little bit to set it up, but once you set it up and get it going, oh my. If you're a local business, it's incredible. Very powerful.

Finding Potential Joint Venture Partners

When you're looking for "JV" partners, you're basically looking for areas of "customer overlap."

Remember the examples above: Subway/gas stations; McDonald's /supermarkets; Wendy's/truck stops.

People who are buying gas on their way home from work can now pick up a couple of sandwiches without having to make a separate stop.

A parent going to a supermarket to buy diapers can get the kids a couple of Happy Meals at the same time.

A truck driver can grab a couple of cheeseburgers and some fries after topping off with diesel. He (or she) doesn't have to sit and wait at a traditional sit down diner, nor pull the rig off to the side of the road because it won't fit in the drive-thru lane.

If you have two things to do, and you can do them both at the same place at almost the same time, that's good.

Customer overlap.

There's a real estate agent in Texas who does a monthly electronic newsletter for people who have bought a home from him—and people he hopes will buy from him someday.

He has joint ventures going with restaurants, dry cleaners, auto lube shops, even a bookstore or two. His newsletter includes links to pages on his website that offer discount coupons his subscribers can print up.

Of course, his name and logo are prominently displayed on the coupons.

Plus, there's a plastic fish bowl at each of the places where he has joint venture arrangements. Every month he offers a prize of some sort that new subscribers can win in a drawing. Usually, the prize is donated by one of the joint venture partners in exchange for a premium plug in his newsletter. That's his incentive for getting people to sign up.

It's a win-win. The restaurants, dry cleaners, quick lube shops, and bookstores get their names in front of targeted customers. The real estate agent enjoys that benefit too, and also keeps his name top-of-mind with clients and prospects alike.

But it doesn't stop there. In the newsletter he also:

- spotlights an attractive property or two that has become available
- promotes seminars and workshops on home financing/home buying that he's conducting
- prints a recipe
- recommends a book he's recently read that he enjoyed (which, of course, you can get at a discount—with the coupon from his website—at the bookstore he's joint venturing with).

Pretty imaginative, huh?

OK, so you're not a real estate agent. But we just wanted to offer this example to show you how you can creatively mine online gold with an offline shovel.

Apply the principles to your product or profession accordingly.

The "Refund Letter" as a Joint Venture Strategy

Here's another tactic suggested by Alex Mandossian that can help you turn "lemons" into "lemonade."

In this case, he partnered up with Armand Morin, who has the *gogenerator.com* line of products — *headergenerator, ecovergenerator,* and *ebookgenerator.*

Alex uses this technique when he gets a refund request from a customer.

> Gosh, refunds sting. They hurt. You dated the prospect with your autoresponder sequence. You began dating them exclusively when they subscribed to your newsletter. They purchased something from you — you got married; they may have bought something else from you, which is like having children. This is a relationship. It's rapport building. You seduced them, and now you have kids.
>
> All of a sudden, they want a divorce. A refund.
>
> What is that? That's customer defection. They return a product. That happens to me, and I get maybe one return per month. I'm very, very fortunate. It's like one half of one percent of the books that I sell. However, it is $247.00, so it's a lot of money.
>
> So here's what happens.
>
> I take that personally. I take it personally because I think, 'Oh my gosh, I did all this and I thought I gave as much value as I could. I'd rather they hadn't purchased the course in the first place, because now it's created a headache for both of us.
>
> But, I have to honor my lifetime guarantee, and it IS good for life. They can give me any reason they want. They can tell me they never opened the box and I'm still going to honor it.
>
> So when they ask for a refund I ask their permission, as I do on the website, to send them a refund check. If they tell me, 'No please credit my credit card,' I'm obliged to do that. But

I prefer refund checks, and 99% of the people want refund checks, believe it or not. They don't mind.

So I send them a letter. There's a cover letter and there's a refund check. It says,

'Dear Mr. Doe. Enclosed you will find a $247.00 refund check as per my unconditional money back guarantee.

Although I realize our paths may never cross again, I do want to introduce to another marketer who can provide you with proven e-business tools for marketing successfully on the net. His name is Armand Morin, and I've made special arrangements with him to allow you to subscribe to his Internet Marketing Tips newsletter for a full year at no cost. I hope you will accept this gesture as a token of my appreciation for giving my Marketing with Postcards course a fair try.

I rarely take the time to write a note like this. But during those rare instances when I get a refund request like yours, I feel morally obliged to refer you to another top marketer who can fulfill your needs.'

The embedded command there of course is 'another top marketer.' I'm inferring that I'm one, too, so I had to put that in there.

'Here is the special web page to pick up your one-year free subscription. www.gogenerator.com/alex Yes! Hand signed. Now what happens when they go to www.gogenerator.com/ alex? If they buy anything for the next 33 years from Armand Morin, I will get a commission. You know what I've just done? I have just offset the $247 refund. Now isn't that an elegant way to get money back?

That's one small example of how two marketers can set up a joint venture.

But most joint ventures offer a much larger appeal.

When partners, each with his or her own big list, form an alliance and promote each other to their respective customers, the results tend to be large — and lucrative.

With big dollars—and credibility—riding on these joint ventures, each partner needs to have considerable faith in the other.

That kind of faith is hard to establish through websites, emails, or even telephone conversations.

"You need to meet your partner in person," says Frank Garon. "You need to be able to look them in the eye. Break bread with them. Make a character judgment."

We don't know that anyone has done an actual study, but experience tells us more joint venture partnerships begin at seminars and workshops than anywhere else.

Remember Jason's Potash's "round robin" teleseminar?

It sprang from a MasterListbuilder workshop in San Antonio in October of 2002.

There are dozens of other examples we could cite.

The Internet may seem sterile and faceless to some people. But to those who use it as a vehicle to make money, it's anything but.

Chapter 12
Business Cards, Civic Organizations, Barter Groups and Trade Associations

Business Cards

You read earlier about some of the ways you can use business cards to build your list when you attend a seminar.

Let's take a look at their potential now in a broader context.

There are entire "how-to" books written about the art and science of passing out business cards at networking events, business meetings, even at parties or other social gatherings.

Obviously it's important. There's no sense dwelling on it.

However, for the list-builder, there's one principle to follow that most other publications are unlikely to mention.

Besides doing all the things everyone else recommends on the front of the card, we recommend putting something extremely important on the back of the card: an invitation to subscribe to your list.

The invitation would be similar to a classified ad you might place in someone else's e-zine. There are several crucial elements:

- It should be quick enough to read in about five seconds.
- It should mention the one or two most important benefits someone can get by subscribing.
- It should include your URL and a call to action, and
- If possible, it should contain an incentive to subscribe, like a free report or free e-book.

For instance:

> Subscribe to George McKenzie's "Get Free Publicity" e-zine
> and receive a 5-day mini-course on how to get thousands of
> dollars worth of free publicity. www.get-free-publicity.com

Of course, you have another option.

Instead of an invitation to subscribe, offer an opportunity to get
something free: a free report, a free e-book, or anything that's likely
to get them to go to your website or a special web page.

Once again, you're giving them repeated opportunities to sign up.
The more you offer, the more likely they are to accept.

For a great primer on other basics of good business card marketing
principles by Raleigh Pinskey, visit

www.get-free-publicity.com/businesscards.htm

Civic Organizations

A lot of people are attracted to marketing online because they'd prefer NOT to market offline. They may be naturally shy, so they prefer
to deal with other people from the relative anonymity of the Internet,
rather than getting out to "glad-hand and backslap" at traditional
networking organizations like the local Chamber of Commerce.

Be that as it may, there's no doubt you can meet a lot of people in a
relatively short period of time by networking in Chambers and civic
organizations like Rotary, Lions, etc.

Here are some simple ideas for maximizing the time (and membership dues) you'll spend marketing in such groups.

Maximize your participation in events and limit your involvement in projects

It's only fair that you should do some of the "grunt work" in
planning/study committees and so on. But if you're one of those
folks who has trouble saying "no" when you're asked to volunteer for
something, you could find yourself spending a lot of time in activities that produce little in the way of results.

You'll have more success in these groups if you focus on attending
events where large numbers of the membership will be showing up.

Move around meeting people, getting to know what they do, and analyzing their potential as subscribers—or centers of influence who can connect you to a group of potential subscribers.

Offer to MC or moderate events and large gatherings.
Look for opportunities to play a speaking role that gets you in front of as many people as possible. If someone else is introducing you, make sure they include the fact that you publish your own newsletter AND that you have however-many-thousand subscribers (assuming of course, that you really do).

Offer your products and services as a door prize where appropriate
We're assuming, of course, that you're probably giving away digital products or low cost self-publications. Many networking breakfasts and lunches conclude with a door prize drawing.

Offer workshops and classes to members
If you can offer some legitimate expertise on something members are interested in, don't hesitate to propose a workshop or a seminar. You'll have to make a judgment call here though—Chamber executives, for instance, are always being approached by "experts" who really want to use these gatherings as "shill shops" in which they shamelessly push their own products and services.

If you portray yourself as a resource rather than a vendor (just as you would with the media), you'll be more successful getting yourself in front of prospects.

Take full advantage of publications
Get to know the editor of the group's newsletter. Treat him or her as if they were no different than the editor of a large local newspaper. Offer articles, tip sheets, expert advice, etc. You may want to consider advertising in the newsletter if that option is available.

Accessing the group's database
Most organizations now publish a directory or member database—including fax numbers and email addresses. This is a huge 'spamming" temptation for some folks.

Definitely seek the guidance of organization leaders executives before sending out mass mailings—by snail mail, email, or fax.

Barter Groups

You won't find these companies everywhere, but if there's one near you, it can be a solid source of free publicity and subscribers for your list.

Barter companies are composed of businesses that are willing to trade goods and services with each other. No cash changes hands.

Usually you pay a modest one-time fee to sign up, and then you pay a percentage of every transaction (whether you're the buyer or the seller) each month.

This may or may not fit your business model. But it's how you can use the barter company for free advertising that could be valuable to you as a list owner.

Here's why.

Since the barter company makes a little money on each transaction, it's in their best interest to promote activity through their members.

There are a number of vehicles they use to do it, and each gives you a chance to get people to your website and then sign up for your list.

Newsletters

Each month, most barter companies send a flyer or a newsletter along with their invoices. These flyers or newsletters announce new companies that have joined the co-op in the last month, and invite members to start trading with them.

But very often, there aren't enough newbies to fill the entire flyer, so the barter company will give the space to anyone who wants to make a special to offer other members.

This gives you the opportunity to set up a special web page just for those who want to check out the deal. When they come to that page, of course, you have the opportunity to turn them into subscribers.

"Trade Flashes"

Many barter companies now have their own opt-in lists, and they email their members three or four times a week offering limited-time special deals. For example, in San Antonio, they'll often send out an email saying something like

Joe Spurs Fan has two tickets to tonight's game at the SBC Center, but his wife's going to have a baby and he's willing to give them up for 80 barter credits. Call your account exec right away before someone else gets them.

There doesn't have to be an emergency. You can make a special, limited time offer for any reason, and get your name in front of hundreds of other barter members, almost on demand.

Fairs, Mixers and Other Events

Several times a year, barter companies generally sponsor social events or trade fairs. You can socialize at the mixers, and set up a booth at the trade fairs.

Marketing to Trade Associations

Do you like to fish?

Even if you don't, there's one principle every fisherman (and fisherwoman) knows that applies to marketing.

No matter how tempting—even irresistible—your bait is, you won't catch anything if you drop your line where there's nothing to catch.

In marketing, this principle is called "targeting."

We can't think of a better example of targeting than this one from Randy Sparage, a former sportscaster at KMOL TV in San Antonio, and later with Fox Southwest.

When Randy was a youngster he played for a Little League team that sold chocolate bars to raise money.

Randy was a top-notch sales person because, even as a child, he understood the importance of targeting the market.

As Randy tells it,

> *Back then we sold the bars for one dollar. But there was a coupon on the wrapper for two dollars off at Pizza Hut. So I'd go down to my local Pizza Hut, approach people as they were about to walk in, and make them a deal.*

'I'll sell you this $2.00 off coupon for $1.00,' I said. 'And I'll even throw in a free chocolate bar you can have for dessert.'

Everybody jumped at the deal.

Great idea, and a great example of targeted marketing.

Which brings us back to the topic of this chapter: marketing to associations.

Let's go back to our fishing analogy for a moment.

When you advertise through the mass media, or even when you put a website on the Internet, it's like dropping a line in the ocean. Yes, there are a LOT of fish out there, but there's also a lot of space. No matter how tightly you target your commercials or optimize your website for the search engines, you're still putting your offer in a place where motivated prospects may never see it.

That's why associations are so attractive. You know what their members are interested in; otherwise they wouldn't be part of the association.

So it's more like dropping your line in a barrel full of fish. Your chances of catching something skyrocket.

There are more than twenty thousand associations in the United States, and about seven thousand in the United Kingdom. Most are tightly focused on one area of interest, or "niche."

As O.J. Simpson's attorney, Johnny Cochran, would probably say, "Scratch the niche and you'll get rich."

Once you know which associations fit your niche, here's how to "start scratching."

Promote your website

Almost all associations have a newsletter or even a press room on their website. Find out the name of the editor or decision-maker and send a press release summarizing how your site can be a valuable resource to association members. If practical, customize a page for the association (see more on this possibility below).

Write articles

Offer articles you've written that would be appropriate for the newsletter. Customize them if possible.

David Frey of www.marketingbestpractices.com experienced outstanding success by writing articles in one of his niches, the pool and spa industry.

Last year I went to Phoenix to this international pool & spas expo. And I stopped by one of the trade magazine booths and just said, 'Hi I'm Dave Frey and I'm a professional marketer. I just created a marketing system for the industry and I can write some articles for you.'

The woman in the booth told me to come back at 4:00 and talk to their editor. I said okay. So I walked away and thought for a moment, you know, I need to do something. So I ran across the street over to Kinko's got on their computer and I typed up probably about 6 different potential articles with headlines and descriptions of what the articles would include. It was 2 pages... just a little letter to the editor introducing myself and offering to do these articles.

I made about 6 copies of those and I personalized each one. So I went back to the Trade Show met with the guy at 4:00 and I gave him his and he just loved it. I did an article for him a month later.

Then I went to some other booths and met with other editors.

Here's an inquiry letter David used to send to other trade association publications.

While it's specific to the pool and spa industry, the concepts and principles will work for just about anyone.

Contact Information:
David Frey
CEO, Marketing Best Practices Inc.
4755 Widerop Lane
Friendswood, Texas 77546

281.993.5657
email: David@MarketingBestPractices.com

To: Managing Editors
Date: December 2, 2002
Subject: Feature Article Inquiry Letter

Dear Managing Editor

I would like to respectfully submit the following feature article ideas to you for consideration. Each topic is an extract from my new spa and pool marketing manual titled: 'Recession-Proof Your Spa and Pool Business: How to Get Business to Come to You', which will be located at www.SpaPoolSucess.com

Article Idea # 1: 'Education-Based Marketing: How to Make Business Come to You.'

Today, spa and pool marketers are facing a different type of prospect as a result of the information revolution. Prospects have become immune to 'selling' messages and are turned off to hard sell tactics. What prospects are thirsting for is not another sales message, but good information that will edu-cate them about their spa and pool choices. Implementing an Education-Based Marketing program will capture spa and pool prospects earlier in the decision process and establish a relationship of trust, resulting in dramatically higher sales and closing ratios. This article will introduce the process of Educa-tion-Based Marketing in the spa and pool industry.

Article Idea # 2: 'Niche-Marketing: Expanding Your Spa and Pool Prospect Base By Narrowing Your Marketing Focus.'

With the imminent threat of a recession and a slowing economy, the same number of spa and pool owners is chas-ing fewer and fewer customers. The ability to proactively seek out new prospects has become vitally important. Tightly focusing marketing efforts on high-probability prospects in niche markets will allow spa and pool owners to significantly expand their prospect base. Additional benefits of niche mar-keting include higher closing ratios as a result of directly ad-

dressing the needs and wants of spa and pool prospects. This article will explain how to implement an effective spa and pool niche-marketing program.

Article Idea # 3: 'Five Strategies for Recession-Proofing Your Spa and Pool Business.'

The slowing economy and recessionary signs have forced spa and pool businesses to re-think their marketing strategies. This article will introduce five proven marketing strategies for recession-proofing a spa and pool business. The five marketing strategies include, (1) Education-Based Marketing, (2) Follow-Up Marketing, (3) Niche-Marketing, (4) Internet Marketing, and (5) Guarantee Marketing.

Article Idea # 4: 'Increase Your Advertising Response Rate Using Cutting-Edge Advertorials.'

Studies have shown that consumers read editorial articles seven times more than traditional advertising. Successful direct response marketers have known this fact for years and as a result, have developed advertisements that both advertise and provide news simultaneously. These types of advertisements are referred to as 'advertorials,' and are extremely powerful in capturing reader's attention — while subtly selling the benefits of a spa and pool business. This article will inform spa and pool owners about how to increase their advertising response rates by up to 700% using advertorials in their marketing mix.

Article Idea # 5: 'Five Secrets to Making Your Website 'Pre-Sell' Like Crazy'

How would you like your prospects to purchase a spa or pool from you on their first visit to your store? It's possible with a dynamic 'pre-selling' website. This article will introduce and explain the five critical elements that will make your website pre-sell like crazy. These website elements are, (1) Powerful headlines, (2) Benefit-laden copy, (3) Information-packed articles, (4) Social proof, and (5) an email-capturing process.

Article Idea # 6: 'Improve Your Spa and Pool Closing Ratio Using Follow-Up Marketing.'

Studies have shown that prospects visit an average of three spa and pool stores before they decide on a purchase. Developing and implementing a structured spa and pool Follow-Up Marketing program is critical to increasing closing ratios. Using new tools and technologies, spa and pool owners can put their Follow-Up Marketing program on autopilot. This article addresses the Follow-Up Marketing process and introduces new tools such as contact management software and email autoresponders to automate the follow-up process.

I would be happy to write a column based on any one (or all) of these six topics. No remuneration is expected; all I would ask is if you would be so kind as to include my resource box at the end of the column.

Thank you for this opportunity to contribute to your magazine. I look forward to hearing from you soon.

David Frey

CEO Marketing Best Practices Inc

Join the association.
This will keep you up to date on trends and developments in the industry. It will also qualify you to get a membership directory, which could be an invaluable marketing tool.

Visit a discussion board or forum
If the association has a discussion board or forum, visit it often to find out what members are talking about. If they have needs you can fill, make contributions, offer articles, tips, survey results, etc.

Speak at events
Market yourself as a speaker at association events.

Talk to the association about sponsoring your website.
They'll get higher visibility among non-association visitors, and perhaps get some new members from it. You'll get the benefit of the "halo effect" — in other words, your connection to the association in this way will give you increased credibility throughout the industry.

Develop a "champion" or an "angel" in the association

Connect with someone who will promote you to other members and spread the word about you as a resource to industry movers and shakers. Remember... association executives are very different from many other corporate leaders. They willing share information with each other, and often seek each other's advice. Word-of-mouth endorsement may be more important among association execs that any other group.

Attend Association Shows

There's no better way to network and keep up to date with industry trends and information. Shows are also excellent opportunities to generate free publicity for you and for the association itself (which, of course, makes you a hero to trade association members.) For an excellent primer, see Joan Stewart's *Special Report #24: How to Create Media Publicity at Trade Shows and Conferences.* It offers advice on

- What media people want to find at trade shows
- How to contact the media instead of waiting for them to contact you
- Little extras you can offer that will make your booth stand out from all the others
- What to do if you're attending a conference but don't have a booth and want publicity

Go to www.get-free-publicity.com/publicityhound.html

There are lots of fish in the marketing ocean. Thanks to associations, many of those fish swim together in schools. Drop your line among them and you dramatically increase your chances of bringing home a nice catch.

See Appendix D for Trade Association resources.

Chapter 13

How to Do Well by Doing Good: Generating Traffic and Profits Through Community Involvement

You've heard the saying a gazillion times: "Charity begins at home."

But in this age of mass media, charity that begins at home can also proceed straight to your bottom line—by generating traffic to your website or your business.

And best of all, the mass media—especially the news media—are ready, willing, and more than able to partner with you.

Charity events and stories about community involvement appeal to the media for a number of reasons.

1. They're very sensitive to criticism that they only want to show bad news, and will make every effort to show uplifting, positive stories whenever possible.
2. It's in their best interest to build goodwill by taking part in community events.
3. In the case of radio and TV stations, they MUST show that they're serving the community. Otherwise, their FCC license would be in jeopardy.
4. For the most part (there are exceptions), they're good-hearted people who really do WANT to help others.

Fundraisers and events that benefit the community amount to a win-win-win situation. Obviously, the charity gets money and attention to their cause, the station or newspaper gets points for its community spirit, and you get publicity that would have cost you thousands of dollars if you had to pay for it.

So, when you want to generate new traffic or more traffic to your business or website, consider creating a fundraiser for a charity or community organization.

Co-op with a Media Sponsor

You can guarantee some enthusiastic coverage for an event if you can work a "co-op" or even find a media backer. Many TV stations, radio stations and newspapers will agree to help you by being a sponsor. Sometimes they offer free advertising, but they might even offer cash to help cover the sponsoring organization's expenses.

Keep in mind that they're besieged each year with sponsorship re-quests. The key to getting exposure is to offer them a lot of exposure in return. That might mean a huge banner or big signs at your event.

If you can give the names and addresses of everyone who buys a tick-et to the newspaper's circulation department (for telemarketing), you make yourself more attractive to them. Some organizations won't be comfortable with this technique, but we'll let you be the judge.

You can also attract media backing by making sure their logo or marketing slogan is included on every piece of your marketing mate-rial.

Understand up front that in most cases, you shouldn't expect much help, if any, with the actual event planning. And don't *assume* you'll get more publicity from that media outlet than you might get oth-erwise. As we explained earlier, news operations safeguard their independence and are particularly sensitive to getting a "push" from other departments.

Nonetheless, it's a good thing to get any help you can from someone who already has a pool of viewers, listeners, or readers who might attend your event.

Different Media, Different Hooks

Different media will look for different things before they'll give you air time or print space.

TV

It almost goes without saying that since television is a visual medium; it helps to do something visual.

When we say visual, we mean three things: people, color, and motion.

People

Obviously, the more people you can get together, the better. If you can get a few famous people, that's best of all (see below).

True, it gives the event more of a sense of importance, but that's not the only reason it's helpful.

The more people you have at the scene when a camera crew shows up, the more people will be likely to go home and watch that night. Many of those people might even call their friends and tell them to watch.

TV stations like that *a lot.*

Color

When we say there should be color, we're not talking all the colors of the rainbow. We're talking about something that's visually appealing or interesting to look at.

Motion

The people who are there should be doing something. In fact, they should be doing something interesting, if possible.

Think about it. How many news stories have you ever seen where a bunch of folks were just milling around with their hands in their pockets? Pictures like that rarely make their air.

Here's an example of a great fundraiser that incorporates all of those elements as well as any event we've ever seen. Call it *The Lipton Dip.*

Several years ago, Church's Chicken franchisee Scott Gross did this one in the parking lot of his restaurant in Kerrville, Texas.

Scott got a local pool company to erect a small aboveground pool, which they filled with water. Scott's iced tea vendor helped turn the water into a huge vat of tea. A local bank joined in by providing several hundred dollars worth of nickels to dump into the pool. Scott enlisted the help of sororities and fraternities from a nearby college, whose members, on a signal, dove into the pool and started grabbing all the nickels they could. The winning fraternity or sorority got a prize, the charity got a contribution, and Scott—with no cash outlay—got thousands of dollars worth of publicity when several TV stations showed up to cover the contest. Oh, by the way... lots of people who attended the event also bought lunch at Scott's restaurant before they went home.

People, color and motion are big attractions for TV. But there are other techniques you can use which improve your chance of getting on the air.

Texture or Context
When possible, offer the media a story about someone who has benefited from the charity. If you can "humanize" the work the charity is doing—"put a human face on it" so to speak—your chances of getting coverage (that is, publicity) will skyrocket.

Remember, all journalists are in the storytelling business.

Enlist Local Celebrities
It's often a good idea to ask a high profile person from the media to be your honorary chairperson. The better known they are, the more impact they'll have.

Generally, most media outlets have a community service or a community outreach department of some kind. These departments are generally eager to help because they *want* their news anchors or columnists to get out in the community.

In the case of TV stations, there's an additional benefit. Since the station has committed time and effort to cover the event, and because it wants the community to know one of its anchors attended, the story is less likely to be pre-empted by breaking news. If at all possible, the producer will try to find a way to get your story into the newscast.

There is one downside to giving an anchorperson a high profile role in your event, and you should be aware of it. While you may get extensive coverage from one station, you may get no coverage from others. This is a judgment call you'll have to make.

Promoting an Upcoming Event on TV

Getting pre-promotion on the evening news is tough. You might get a mention or two if the station has a "community calendar" segment or "bulletin board" feature, but that's about the best you can hope for until the day of the event itself.

But you do have a good chance of getting pre-promotion on early morning shows, public affairs shows, or magazine shows if you supply as many of the following as possible:

A good spokesperson
If possible, find someone who's comfortable and experienced in front of a camera. This person should also be familiar enough with your event to work date, time, location, and contact information into the conversation not once — but several times.

If you can get a celebrity to make some appearances or do some interviews, you'll be likely to generate more interest both from the media and their audiences.

Video of a previous event
You'll greatly increase your chances of getting pre-event TV coverage if you can offer the station videotape from last year, showing some of the activities that took place, and how all had a good time.

Information
They'll probably ask you for basic information about the event so they can flash it on the screen. Don't leave this to chance however. If they haven't gotten these particulars from you by the day before your appearance, call them and offer it.

Reporter involvement in the story
If you can offer local reporters a chance to do something unique and

report on it, you increase your chances of getting coverage. For instance, an amusement park might invite the media out for a ride on its new roller coaster the day before the park opens.

"Media Day"

San Antonio used to host a grand prix auto race every year. A month or so before the event itself, they'd stage a "media day." They'd take the local sports reporters to a nearby track and let them drive an old racecar. If your event lends itself to such "reporter involvement "(remember photographers too), don't pass up the chance to use it to your advantage.

Promoting on radio

Many of the same principles, strategies, and techniques you'd use for TV apply to radio.

But radio, according to Sonny Melendrez, is "theater of the mind."

Whereas TV creates pictures with videotape, radio creates pictures with words.

"Suppose you're promoting a spaghetti dinner," Sonny says. "By itself—not very exciting. So get creative. Go to the Internet. Look up the history of spaghetti. Talk about how it was really spaghetti—not turkey—that the Pilgrims served at the first Thanksgiving."

You can also talk about different ways spaghetti can be cooked—ways you never thought of.

Always be aware of the tone of the show and the personality of the host. Some will let you "get away" with more than others. Also keep in mind the news of the day. If something grim has happened recently, it will be less appropriate to get wild and crazy.

But have fun—just make sure you don't have so much fun that you forget to mention (several times) date, time, location, and cause.

Promoting in Print

A media kit is a must for both broadcast and print, but it's especially important for newspapers.

Media kits that promote an event are somewhat different than kits that promote an individual or a company. And there's no need for razzle-dazzle. Concentrate on content, not flash, especially if you're trying to keep expenses down and turn over a bigger check to a charity.

Here are some things to include. These should also be available on a website, if possible.

- A history of the event, including how, when, and why it started, along with who started it.
- Fun facts about the fund-raiser through the years. How much money has been raised?
- A fact sheet: locations, prices, special guests and other details the media will need to know.
- A map showing the layout and how to get there. Highlight the media parking area.
- A schedule of activities.
- A camera-ready logo.
- A list of key contacts — not just the publicity chairperson. List alternates too. Include home and work telephone numbers as well as cell phone numbers.
- Photos and bios of any celebrities who will be there. You should also work with the celebrities' publicity staff to arrange media interviews a week or so before the event.

Finally, while most newspaper stories will be done in printed words, don't overlook photo possibilities. If you have pictures or slides from previous events, make sure to include them in your media kit. We've all heard that a picture is worth a thousand words — and it's true that a colorful or attractive picture can draw as many people to your event as a printed article.

Choosing a Charity to Help

Before you read the section that follows, let's get something on the record.

We're not suggesting you choose a charity based solely on its media-appeal. We believe you should follow your heart, with input from those who will help you put the event or campaign together.

Consider community needs, and the impact you can have on the lives of those you're trying to help.

But, that said, you should also understand that certain TV stations, radio stations, and print media often become "angels" of one or two organizations. While they certainly work with others, they focus much of their effort—and airtime or print space—toward helping a fortunate few favorites.

This is critical to remember, because if a media outlet is committed to a certain cause, it will make every effort to promote that cause—short of selling out its journalistic integrity.

For instance, if there are two charity events scheduled for coverage in a newscast, but there's only time enough to mention one because of breaking news, guess which one will get on the air?

Once again, doing some intelligence work is important. Watch, listen, and read with an awareness of who's covering which charities and how much airtime or print space they get.

Or you can do something easier than that.

Call the community service departments and ask which charities they work with most often. Also ask for a contact name at that organization, and then approach that contact.

Very often, the contact will actually help you get coverage, and he or she might even get some of their volunteers to assist you in organizing and staffing the event. Those volunteers might even go to the event themselves, which swells your attendance and makes your event more attractive and newsworthy.

Make Your Event "Media-Friendly"

Timing your event will also have a huge impact on your success with the media. Try to make sure it doesn't compete with another major event in your community. Call your local Chamber of Commerce or Convention & Visitors Bureau for help on this.

Schedule your "media opportunities" with flexibility in mind. Remember that many journalists cover more than one event in the course of a day, and breaking news sometimes might throw them off schedule. If it's possible to make the timing of your event or "photo op" flexible, you increase your chances of success.

Plan every activity of your event so that it appeals to the media. Give them something to report on besides milling crowds. At the annual Cowboy Breakfast in San Antonio (an event that attracts fifty thousand people at 6:30 AM every year), they start breaking eggs for the tacos the day before. A pile of several thousand eggshells makes an interesting visual for TV or even still photos.

Several years ago the Cowboy Breakfast scored a huge coup when organizers, working with the local NBC affiliate, attracted The Today Show's Willard Scott to do his weather report live. Scott also agreed, as part of the gig, to attempt to throw a "cow patty" into a toilet bowl from about 25 yards away. Incredibly, he scored a "bulls-eye" on national TV (Einstein would have trouble calculating the aerodynamics of a flying cow-patty, but Scott "swished it" it on the first try.) His success resulted in a round of one-liners from the Today Show hosts, priceless attention across the country, and a memorable video moment on the local news that night. Even the ABC and CBS affiliates showed it.

Don't forget the small things, like reserved media parking. If the media has to use public parking, and a TV photographer, for instance, has to lug 30 pounds of equipment a quarter of a mile to cover you, you can bet the assignment editor will hear about it when the photographer returns to the station. You can also bet the assignment editor will make a mental note of it.

Remember too that most media outlets will make one visit only. So if you have a multi-day event, try to get them to come on the first day, when the most interesting things are planned. Good coverage on opening day will help boost attendance for rest.

One of our friends used to sign off his show every day by telling his listeners this:

"Remember, do good and you'll always do well." It's true in life. It's especially true when you want to get free publicity in the media.

Need more tips on how to pitch by letter, phone or e-mail? Each method of pitching has its own problems and benefits. For more help, check out these special reports:

#7: *How to Write the Perfect Pitch Letter That Convinces an Editor to Write About You*

#16: *How to Write Tip Sheets That Catch the Media's Attention*

#18: *Clever Contests That Will Tempt Reporters to Call*

#19: *How to Use Polls, Surveys and White Papers That Brand You as an Expert*

#26: *How to Make Your Story Pitch Stand Out in the E-mail Jungle*

Dozens of tips for only $9.00 per report. Order at www.get-free-publicity.com/publicityhound.html

Once again, you can get a great deal more depth on this topic in *How to Plan and Promote Sizzling Special Events* by Joan Stewart and Debra J. Schmidt.

It's a series of six audiocassettes and 5 valuable checklists that offer 847 tips and step-by-step details on how to make your next event a huge success.

Joan and Debra also give you a download of three of their checklists for free. Go to www.get-free-publicity.com/publicityhound.html for more information.

Conclusion

Here's one of our favorite quotes. Unfortunately, neither of us knows who said it, but we certainly believe it's true.

"Genius is not a matter of doing one thing one hundred percent better than everyone else. It's a matter of doing one hundred things one percent better than everyone else."

That's how we view list-building.

If you consistently do a lot of little things your competitors aren't, they're going to add up. They'll have a cumulative effect, and it won't be long before you're way ahead of them—and possibly way ahead of everyone else.

That said, don't hesitate to look for ways to work with your competition on suitable joint ventures.

This is the principle of "coopetition." You each bring an asset of value to the alliance that the other doesn't have. In the case of list-building, it's a pool of subscribers to which you wouldn't have access otherwise.

Through coopetition, you both benefit.

Finally, don't forget to take advantage of what we call "center-of-influence networking", or COIN. We haven't mentioned it before, but we're planning an entire book on the subject.

Center-of-influence networking involves finding people who can help you grow your business, and recruiting them to do a joint venture with you.

"But why would someone like Marlon Sanders or Frank Garon or Alex Mandossian take time to work with me?" you're probably asking. "I don't have the stature or reputation they do. I'm not nearly at their level."

Don't underestimate yourself. And don't get the wrong impression about people like Marlon, Frank, or Alex. They're open to suggestions from anyone who has something of value to offer in return.

The trick is, figuring what value you can offer them in return, and approaching them a certain way.

That's what our next book will be about.

Remember, building a productive and profitable subscriber or "opt-in" list is a mindset. You look for every opportunity to add subscribers in everything you do—in all your marketing materials, in all your strategies, in all your public appearances, in all your relationships.

Relationships are probably the most important of all.

Frank Garon calls it "bondability." The more you can bond with your subscribers, your customers and your colleagues, the more your business—and your list—will grow.

The strongest relationships are rarely forged online, in the world of "clicks."

They're formed through "bricks"—the offline strategies, tactics, and techniques you use to touch people in physical space, not in cyberspace.

There's a treasure trove of gold to be mined online.

And in years to come, those who mine the most will use an offline shovel.

Appendix A
Media Resources

Lists and Databases of Media Contacts

http://www.radio-locator.com

Links to over 10,000 radio station web pages and over 2500 audio streams from radio stations in the U.S. and around the world. Searchable database.

http://realguide.real.com/tuner

Searchable database of 2500 radio stations.

http://www.tvradioworld.com

TVRadioWorld is an informational directory dealing with the radio and television broadcasters worldwide.

http://www.airwaves.com/fccdb.html

Quick and powerful search engine for the FCC (Federal Communications Commission) Mass Media database of USA and Canadian AM/FM radio stations.

http://www.radio-locator.com/cgi-bin/locate

Use this page to locate all of the radio stations near a U.S. city.

http://100kwatts.tmi.net/

Information about every TV and radio station in the US.

Companies and Individuals Who Write and/or Distribute Press Releases

www.eworldwire.com

Release Distribution from $99 - Includes Online HTML Format.

www.kcwriter.com

Kelle Campbell can help you with your press releases, feature articles, newsletters, business letters, Web pages, and more.

http://www.press-release-writing.com/

Also offers a database of 35,000 journalists and media outlets.

http://www.pressreleasenetwork.com/

An electronic press release distribution service for promoting any business online.

http://www.prweb.com/

Free online press release distribution.

http://mediagoons.com

Press Release Management Software

http://www.xpresspress.com/

Personalized e-mail distribution of press releases to customized media lists internationally.

http://www.internetnewsbureau.com/

Send your press release to more than 10,000 subscribing journalists & business professionals.

http://www.faxaway.com/

Broadcast fax service. Lots of other services are listed on the net and in USA Today.

http://www.globalpresswire.com/

600 publishing partners and news feed recipients for a single annual price of $160.

http://www.submitexpress.com

Distributes direct company news, including press releases, financial announcements, graphics, audio and video files, and other time-critical business communications materials, to a worldwide audience of media, analysts and consumers.

http://www.prwizard.com

The New PRWizard Pro is a powerful, automated press release submission software that lets you effortlessly broadcast your Press Release to over 28,000 targeted Media Contacts.

http://www.onlinepressreleases.com

Producers of "Media Magnet" software. With four easy steps you can create and send out a press release to over 28,000 media contacts. You can submit and resubmit your site as often as you like. You can also create your own list from your contacts.

Publicity Products

Joan Stewart's Special Reports

Secrets of Speed Publicity by Marlon Sanders

How To Get Booked On Oprah by Susan Harrow

Power Publicity by Rick Beneteau and Anne Marie Baugh

Alex Carroll's Radio Publicity System Alex Carroll

How To Promote Your Local Business On The Internet! by Sharon Fling

Appendix B
Publishing Resources

Tom Antion's "Product Development" audio cassette, available through Tom's "Speaker Shop" on his website. See the "Kick Series Teleseminar Audio Tapes" section at http://www.get-free-publicity.com/speakershop.html

Marlon Sanders explains how it's now possible to create products even if you don't have much expertise in your field and aren't good at writing. He calls his program "Create Your Own Products in a Flash". http://www.get-free-publicity.com/createproducts.html

Joe Vitale and Jim Edwards offer *How To Write And Publish an eBook In As Little As 7 Days*. The authors say they can show you how to do it "even if you can't write, can't type and failed high school English class." http://www.get-free-publicity.com/7dayebook.html

Armand Morin's "eCoverGenerator" will give your e-book a three-dimensional, professional "publishing house look." Use your own graphics and artwork, or choose from over 150 templates provided with the program. http://www.get-free-publicity.com/o/ecovergenerator.html

If you want a customized cover at a very reasonable price, simply hand over the design work to Vaughan Davidson. http://www.get-free-publicity.com/kilcovers.html

Appendix C
Fax Resources

Fax Marketing Corporation

Ron Ressler operates this company and Yanik Silver says in How To Make Instant Sales and Immediate Profits Using Cheap Fax Advertising it's the one he uses for his fax campaigns.

1-800-800-2087 or faxmarket@aol.com

FaxSave

They claim to have more than four million fax numbers in their database.

http://www.faxsave.com/

FindMore Buyers.Com

Over 5.4 million companies are available in the U.S. alone. Their website claims they target the specialized segments of the market that matches your 'best customer' demographics.

http://findmorebuyers.com

HomeGrown Advertising Inc.

Website says they have 5.5 million fax listings across North America, and they can send up to 350,000 faxes per hour

http://www.express-advertising.com/

WorldWide Marketing

A division of CYNET (see below). They offer lists for sale for less than .10 per name.

281-897-8317

http://www.cynetinc.com/

Fax Broadcast Companies

CYNET

Fax broadcasting, desk-top fax, fax to email, email to fax, and email broadcasting. Brand new to the line-up, is our CYNET Remove Me service, allowing for easy removal for unsolicited recipients when performing mass distributions. Additionally, for marketers, through CYNET's subsidiary World Wide Marketing Services (WWMS), clients are able to purchase targeted e-Marketing list and data.

http://www.cynetinc.com/

DeMayo Mail Management

Lists, Directories & Printing/Mailing Services

http://www.demayo.com/printmail/

Fax4Free

You can receive faxes for free—however, there's a charge for sending them. But, the company says there's no need for special computer equipment, expensive fax boards, special software, multiple phone lines or the inconvenience of outsourcing.

http://www.fax4free.com

listsareus.com

45,000 lists available in just about any category you can imagine http://listsareus.com/

Launchfax

http://www.launchfax.com

NetMoves

Lets you send and receive faxes right from your e-mail.

http://www.netmoves.com/cgi-bin/netmovesoffercgi

Xpedite

Offers electronic document distribution and data messaging including fax, e-mail, voice and wireless.

http://www.xpedite.com

Fax Software

Winfax

We've personally used this Symantec product. The learning curve was steeper than some other stuff we've used, but we were able to figure it out and start faxing in a relatively short period of time. We appreciated the fact that we were able to upload an existing ACT database into it seamlessly, and set it up to fax out literally hundreds of flyers overnight.

http://www.symantec.com/winfax/

Appendix D
Trade Association Resources

Here are some trade association websites and resources you may find helpful:

The School of Association Management Online: http://desktopasae.certilearn.com/

The Virtual Law School offers six courses on non-profit law and legal issues: http://www.asaenet.org/courses/1,1806,50766,00.html

Association Management: Essentials of the Profession™ features print-based study modules and testing exercises on CD-ROM. It features a complete learning system covering all disciplines of association management. http://www.asaenet.org/essentials

There are also knowledge network at http://www.asaenet.org/education/roundtables and frequent seminars and symposia you can access to build your expertise.

About the Authors

Joel Christopher

Joel Christopher, The MasterListBuilder, is the Director and Owner of SuccessAccess.com, The Success Consultants.

In the late 90s, he started using the Internet as a way to keep in touch with his family and business associates. Recognizing the business and marketing potential of the Internet, he started his own online business in late 1999 and launched it on January 1, 2000.

Finding no website at the time that was geared towards providing a step-by-step guide to succeeding online for aspiring Internet Entrepreneurs, he created one.

SuccessAccess.com exists to offer 'Beginner Internet Marketers' and 'Newbie Netpreneurs' a step-by-step Internet business success guide to starting, growing and expanding your own online business.

As a Licensed Physical Therapist for 13 years prior to becoming a full-time Netpreneur, Joel did not have any writing, marketing or technical background. Frustrated that he could not find a website that was "Newbie-Friendly", he started SuccessAccess.com to help Newbie Netpreneurs and internet marketing beginners succeed online.

He has built and grown his own email subscriber list to more than 100,000 subscribers. During one three-month period in 2001, he tripled his list from 10,000 to more than 30,000.

International Best-Selling Author and Radio Talk Show Host Mike Litman recently nicknamed him "The Tony Robbins of Internet

Marketing" and Randy Gilbert of "The Inside Success Show" called him "The Michael Jordan of Internet ListBuilding".

For this reasons, many Internet veterans consider Joel *the* Master ListBuilder Coach.

George McKenzie

George McKenzie is a former professional baseball player turned TV sportscaster and news anchor. During his thirty year broadcasting career, his work has been seen on ABC, CBS, NBC, CNN and ESPN.

George and his wife Dianne also operated a successful chain of Subway Sandwich Shops for nearly ten years.

Because of his experience in professional sports, television news, and small business, George offers a wide range of perspectives to those seeking free advertising and publicity.

For twelve years, he was a highly regarded weeknight sportscaster at KMOL TV in San Antonio Texas, USA, where he won the "Best Sportscast In Texas" Award from the Texas Association Of Broadcasters three times.

George also teaches presentation and communication skills to executives, professionals, and business owners. In addition, he has narrated a number of corporate training videos for a variety of clients, including several for the U.S. Army.

Besides his keynote speeches, media training, and informational programs, George has written several books on how individuals and businesses use the mass media to generate publicity. They include "How To Achieve Massive Profits Through Free Publicity," and "The Instant Press Release Toolkit.

His websites include www.get-free-publicity.com and www.pressreleasetoolkit.com.